CULTURE SHOCK!

Cuba

Mark Cramer

Graphic Arts Center Publishing Company
Portland, Oregon

In the same series

Australia	India	Singapore	London at Your Door
Bolivia	Indonesia	South Africa	Paris at Your Door
Borneo	Ireland	Spain	Rome at Your Door
Britain	Israel	Sri Lanka	
Burma	Italy	Sweden	A Globe-Trotter's Guide
California	Japan	Switzerland	A Parent's Guide
Canada	Korea	Syria	A Student's Guide
Chile	Laos	Taiwan	A Traveller's Medical Guide
China	Malaysia	Thailand	A Wife's Guide
Czech	Mauritius	Turkey	Living and Working Abroad
Republic	Mexico	UAE	Working Holidays Abroad
Denmark	Morocco	USA	
Egypt	Nepal	USA—The	
France	Netherlands	South	
Germany	Norway	Vietnam	
Greece	Pakistan		
Hong Kong	Philippines		

Illustrations by TRIGG
Front cover photograph by The Image Bank
Back cover photograph by Photobank Photolibrary/Singapore
Inside photographs by Mark Cramer unless otherwise stated

© 1998 Times Editions Pte Ltd

This book is published by special
arrangement with Times Editions Pte Ltd
Times Centre, 1 New Industrial Road, Singapore 536196
International Standard Book Number 1-55868-411-5
Library of Congress Catalog Number 98-70217
Graphic Arts Center Publishing Company
P.O. Box 10306 • Portland, Oregon 97296-0306 • (503) 226-2402

Printed in Singapore

To two of my favorite eclectic free spirits:
My son Monty
and
Jonathan Griffiths,
the editor who matched me up with this controversial
project, which has altered the course of my life.

CONTENTS

ACKNOWLEDGEMENTS

My thanks to hundreds of Cubans for sharing ideas with uncompromising frankness and spontaneity, especially Caridad. I'm indebted to Ayesha Ercelawn, my editor, for her meticulous work and sensitive approach to a controversial subject. On more than one occasion, she did informational investigation that most editors would not have found time for, and thus rescued me from factual errors. Trigg's artistic humor will be greatly appreciated by everyone but Uncle Sam. Finally, thanks to my soul partner, Martha Sonia, for having encouraged me to embark on this risky project.

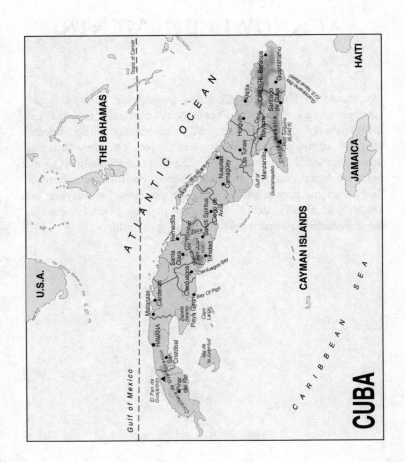

CUBA

U.S.A.

THE BAHAMAS

Tropic of Cancer

Gulf of Mexico

ATLANTIC OCEAN

Cordillera de Guaniguanico
El Pan de Guajaibón
San Cristóbal
Pinar del Río
HAVANA
Isla de la Juventud
Zapata Swamp
Playa Girón
Bay Of Pigs
Cayo Largo
Matanzas
Cárdenas
Cienfuegos
Cienfuegos Bay
Santa Clara
Remedios
San Juan Hill
Sierra de Trinidad
Trinidad
Zaza
Sancti Spíritus
Ciego de Ávila
Camagüey
Nuevitas
Cauto Basin
Las Tunas
Holguín
Gibara
ORIENTE
Baracoa
Cauto
Bayamo
Santiago de Cuba
Guantánamo
Guantánamo Bay (U.S. Naval Base)
Manzanillo
Gulf of Guacanayabo
Sierra Maestra
Pico Turquino (6,540 ft)

CAYMAN ISLANDS

CARIBBEAN SEA

JAMAICA

HAITI

8

INTRODUCTION

Since its 1959 revolution, Cuba has been one of the most controversial countries in the world. My task was to dodge the arguments as best I could and write a non-political narrative that would help the reader integrate within Cuban culture. My approach was simple: I would get intensely involved in the daily life of Cuba and take in a compendium of perceptions and opinions of local inhabitants, foreign residents, non-partial diplomats, and written sources.

This non-partisan approach will inevitably be considered political by both extremes: the United States foreign policy establishment with its Cuban exile lobbyists, and Cuban officialdom. Dominant sectors of the U.S. State Department, the Cuban exile community, and the Cuban government have one thing in common: either you're with 'em or agin' 'em. These two extremes monopolize media coverage of Cuba but represent only a small portion of richly textured Cuban public opinion. Once beyond the extremes, you rarely hear the expected platitudes.

There is a dilemma in transmitting one's experiences with Cuban culture. On the one hand, there is a continuity of culture that would exist regardless of the political system. But overlapping the cultural continuity are profound social transformations stemming from the Cuban Revolution. Whatever happens in Cuba's political future, many of these transformations have become so deeply rooted that they will remain in the Cuban spirit. A sense of the dynamics between centuries-old customs and post-1959 cultural transformations requires a lengthier historical introduction than customary in *Culture Shock!* books.

One prime example is worth introducing at this point. Prior to the revolution, Cuban society was marked by conspicuous class and race distinctions. The revolution changed all that. No longer does one hear the type of linguistic terminologies of social humility still prevalent in much of the rest of Latin America when humble people address their superiors. Even though tourism and the introduction of an independent dollar economy are creating incipient economic divisions, Cubans are unlikely to revert to past customs of addressing others as their social superiors.

As Cuba's national poet, Nicolás Guillén wrote in his classic poem *Tengo* ("I Have"):

> I have the joy of going
> to a bank and talking to the administrator,
> not in English,
> not in sir,
> but simply in *compañero*, as they say in Spanish
>
> I have, let's see,
> that being a black man
> no one will halt me
> at the door of a dance hall or a bar

Independent of whatever political or economic system may emerge in the future, Cubans now have a deeply engrained need for social equality that they will not suddenly abandon.

"There is an organic humanism that is rare in the United States," writes California photographer Adam Kufeld in his book *Cuba*. "Cubans look out for others, whether the stranger is down the block or halfway around the world. Their ethos gives them a consciousness that makes them part of a human family."

THE SPECIAL PERIOD

This "organic humanism" faces its greatest obstacle at the turn of the twenty-first century. The Cuban contradiction of the late 1990s was summed up by a commentator on Radio France International. He noted in late 1997 that the three great achievements of the Cuban revolution were "la education, la santé et les sports," (education, health, and sports) while Cuba's three great problems were "le petit déjeuner, le déjeuner et le diner" (breakfast, lunch, and dinner).

The dramatic scenario of one of the world's best educated populations struggling to survive under socialism after the 1991 implosion of the socialist bloc was bound to create an unprecedented test of will for the nation. Drama is an understatement. Never have I been in a country whose atmosphere of daily life is so charged with powerful and contradictory emotions. No visitor can remain unmoved, and many are moved to bitter-sweet tears that blend sublime joy with overwhelming pathos. On any and every day or night of the year, you may walk out into the streets and experience overlapping feelings of utopian optimism and intense disillusionment.

This is a "Special Period in a time of peace," Fidel Castro's name for an austerity program, initiated since the loss of Soviet subsidies in 1991 and the subsequent escalation of the U.S. trade embargo. Under the Special Period, Cuban people have been asked to bear with severe shortages in food, fuel, and medicines, until Cuban agronomists can expand and diversify food production and the tourism industry can

11

bring in needed foreign currency. Children and the elderly receive extra rations, but everyone else is expected to make ends meet creatively, planting gardens, raising chickens, bartering, using oxen to plow fields, and riding bicycles (given out for free) because there is little gasoline for public transportation.

But one way to make ends meet, unplanned by Fidel, was prostitution.

A young woman, no more than 15 or 16 years old, approaches me one night and in near perfect English resulting from superb schooling, asks me bashfully, "Would you like to come to my room?" Excluded from the dollar economy, she rationalizes that one or two sexual encounters with foreigners can keep her family on an equal footing with those Cubans who receive dollars from Miami. She is not a prostitute in the classic sense. She is *resolviendo,* or making ends meet, during a time of hardship.

The young woman knows how much the *jineteras* (female jockeys) can earn in one trip around the track with a tourist. (Given the substantial disparity in currencies, a $20 trick earns a *jinetera* two months of a doctor's salary, equivalent to a $20,000 trick had the woman earned the same proportional amount in the U.S.)

In this context of an enormous incentive to do an occasional trick, I should be more compassionate in my reaction, but I back off in horror.

"I'm sorry," she says, timidly, after I scold her. "Maybe we can just go out to the Malecón and talk for awhile." (The Malecón is Havana's outdoor, oceanside living room, a city-long stone seawall where neighbors chat, hustlers sell cigars, children dive into the water, men catch a fish dinner, and occasionally, a professional woman seeks a liaison with an affluent tourist to complement her meager salary.)

Olga Gasaya, vice-chair of the Department of Psychology at the University of Havana believes that the "resurgence of prostitution is connected to the economic crisis. Although the crisis affects most women to the same degree, all women look for different ways to solve it, and only a small percentage of them resort to prostitution."

Gasaya's analysis was substantiated, to the benefit of my emotional sanity, when I met another young woman, another potential victim of the Special Period, whose resolute idealism prevents her from yielding to the temptation to earn dollars in a humiliating way.

Soledad, whom we shall meet in later pages, is a 22-year-old lady friend with a utopian view of social equality, who chooses the usual rice and beans over a piece of tasty chicken because she laments not sharing the hard-to-get delicacy with her neighbors and family.

The visitor who does not want to remain cloistered in a hotel room has no choice but to take this ride of contradicting emotions. Cubans are quick to bare their feelings and they expect you to respond to probing questions as if you'd known them their whole lives. Given the hardships, the stories they share with you are apt to be poignantly dramatic, almost always with a sly sense of humor in that uniquely Cuban nasal chant of Spanish.

In Acapulco, Mexico, daredevil divers are a tourist attraction. But here at the Malecón seawall, Havana's outdoor living room, these after-school divers are just part of a great neighborhood.

Fortunately, the hardships have been gradually diminishing. Even as the Special Period and "blockade" continued, the United Nations Human Poverty Index was ranking "Cuba second-best among 78 developing nations," as reported in a 1997 *U.S. News & World Report* article. The index, according to reporter Kevin Whitelaw, was based on "five indicators: literacy, life expectancy, access to health care and safe water, and the percentage of malnourished children."

GOOD HEALTH

Mrs. Vidal, a frequent visitor to Cuba from Spain, suggested to me that perhaps the 76-year life expectancy in Cuba (one year longer than in the U.S.), was precisely due to the fact that Cubans were eating less and not more. "Scientists once experimented with rats," she said, "feeding one group of rats less than another. The group that ate less lived longer."

But public health specialist Howard Waitzkin had more objective ideas about Cuba's relative good health in times of deprivation. According to him, the scarcity of red meat had evidently led to lower rates of hyperlipidemia, and the escalated use of bicycles during oil shortages probably reduced pollution-related maladies, as well as improving the overall physical condition of the Cuban population.

Gina Margillo, a health educator from the United States, visited Cuba to learn about the health care system. Margillo believes that the criteria in the explanations of Vidal and Waitzkin have less impact on Cuban longevity than the country's holistic, interdisciplinary health care methodology, as well as the sense of community and family. "People have an emotional support system," she explained, "which has so much to do with good health."

Mrs. Vidal and her husband, owners of a photography business in Bilbao, Spain, are among the many visitors who fell in love with Cuba and now return frequently with gifts of support. Mrs. Vidal admits that in spite of the hardships, the Cubans have been resilient in maintaining a positive spirit, and continue to master the art of enjoying life.

Photo: Siomara Cramer

Hanging out with friends, practicing the art of conversation: this is Cuba's greatest form of entertainment.

GETTING TO KNOW CUBANS

Cuban pastimes include music and dance, baseball and sports in general, an afternoon on the beach, or a good old-fashioned party. Multi-dimensioned Cubans embrace apparently opposite diversions such as scientific research and eroticism.

But if there is one form of entertainment that most characterizes the Cuban culture, it is hanging out with friends, neighbors, and family (and strangers, too), usually at outdoor public gathering places; this is the social support system that Gina Margillo so admires. When Colombian novelist Gabriel García Márquez asked Fidel Castro in what place he would like to be, Castro responded: "hanging out on some street corner."

For the foreigner, the Cuban way of life is remarkably accessible. Foreign visitors to most countries usually must engage in elaborate methods for integrating within a culture: joining clubs, taking classes, becoming involved in volunteer programs. In Cuba, all of these

15

activities are worthy, but foreigners don't have to make great efforts to find friends. The Cubans will find you.

Even without the benefit of foreign travel, a significant number of Cubans have been schooled to communicate effectively in English. As an experienced language teacher, I find this extraordinary. Rarely in other countries in this hemisphere, excepting bilingual Canada, do high school language courses actually teach students to communicate.

But Cuba remains a predominantly Spanish-speaking country, and a rudimentary knowledge of Spanish will get you a long way in the realm of human relations. Cubans are remarkably patient in dealing with the broken Spanish of a well-meaning visitor.

Cuba is a country of neighborhoods, and the best method for foreigners to become part of the scene is to choose a neighborhood that fits their affinities, and then do plenty of hanging out. By all means branch out and take trips. But establish your turf.

If you do not plan to live in Cuba, you may find, as did Mr. and Mrs. Vidal, that the friends you make on your first visit will draw you back. Most of the people I encounter who have been to Cuba once are lured back for repeat visits.

Should you choose to remain in tourist compounds like Varadero, you'll have a good time for sure, but you'll miss the profound joy of becoming part of a real community. "A person who has come to Varadero has not seen Cuba," declared Cuban architect Miguel Coyula.

THE DOLLAR GAP

There is a critical contrast, more like an unbreachable gap, between a tourist economy in dollars and a local Cuban peso way of life in which small amounts of money are combined with subsidies and bartering in order to get through the month. The average monthly salary in Cuba is only a fraction of what it costs to stay a single night in a Varadero resort hotel. Within the non-tourist economy, a bus ride costs the equivalent of two cents, as does an orange or banana. Cubans are charged only symbolic fees for events like ballet or baseball. The cost to foreigners with dollars is higher, but still considerably less than in other Latin American countries.

The U.S. economic embargo is at least partially to blame, according to most experts (cited later in this text), for a scarcity of certain products, especially medicines. Most affected are those Cubans without access to dollars. This dollar gap, according to California feminist Bethany Leal, "is creating class distinctions that Cubans are not accustomed to." The schizophrenic currency scenario leads to distortions in human relations, including the re-emergence of prostitution, which according to Leal, a frequent visitor to Cuba, "is strictly economics."

Just one symbolic act, that of changing dollars to Cuban pesos, will open up a whole new world to the visitor. Yes, one can get along within the dollar economy, but many of the most typical of Cuban places, both public and private, operate in pesos. Use Cuban pesos and you'll get to know Cuba more while incidentally spending less and eluding scenes around hotels where hustling for scarce dollars is the primary activity.

RACIAL AND SOCIAL EQUALITY

No matter what you think about the Cuban Revolution, and no matter how this country eventually evolves, it can be said that since the early sixties, Cuba has been experimenting, sometimes groping, for ways to create a society in which social equality is the norm. Even with the contradictions of tourism, there is still greater equality among Cubans than one finds within any other Latin American country.

"In Cuba, the highest paid worker can earn only about seven times the salary of the lowest paid worker," writes Kufeld. "It is possible for a hard-working cane cutter to make as much as a doctor. Rationing goods further equalizes things."

Many Cubans who have grown to resent Fidel Castro have something in common with those who love him: they do not want to lose the social advances of the revolution, even if they are highly critical of the revolution in other ways.

Anyone who has ever been in racially divided cities like Washington, D.C. or Chicago, or class-conscious countries like Bolivia or India, or regions of ethnic conflict in Asia, Africa, and Eastern Europe, will marvel at how inter-racial friendships in Cuba have become the norm rather than the exception. Cuba is by no means a utopia of racial harmony, but no other country in the hemisphere enjoys as much social interaction between the racial sectors, which in Cuba are primarily blacks, whites, and mulattos. One of the few remaining complaints about racial imbalance concerned the number of blacks in the highest positions of political power. But following the 1997 party congress elections, blacks were well-represented on the Communist Party central committee.

Ninety miles to the north in Miami, Florida, "black Cuban-Americans find themselves in a bind," writes Mireya Navarro in the *New York Times*. As Cubans they belong to an immigrant group that has enjoyed tremendous economic and political success. But as blacks they have experienced the discrimination and hardships of African-Americans. Blacks in Cuba do not face such obstacles.

"The medical profession [in Cuba], for example, is fully integrated in proportion to the racial distribution of the population, as opposed to the situation before the revolution," according to Dr. Waitzkin. "There is no evidence of racial barriers that inhibit patients' access to diagnostic, curative, or preventive services."

Many visitors to Cuba interviewed for this book agreed that the lack of social inhibitions and an immediate frankness with friends and foreigners alike is a prevailing trait of Cuban culture. Most Cubans have few qualms about sharing intimate feelings or criticizing their leaders, even when they are sitting in a park a few meters from the ubiquitous policemen on every block.

In subsequent chapters, we shall learn what these people have to say.

Chapter One

HISTORY AND SOCIAL SETTING

Before we meet some fascinating characters and partake in Cuba's remarkable human drama, a feel for the social and physical context is essential.

ECONOMICS: A HISTORY OF DEPENDENCE

With the fall of the Soviet Union in 1991, most political analysts predicted a speedy end to Cuba's socialist experiment. They failed to consider national pride, a cultural trait that transcends the avowed Marxism-Leninism of Fidel Castro. Ever since Spain's first settlements on the island in 1512 and the subsequent defeat of Hatuey, the Taino Indian *cacique* (chief) a year later, Cuba's relationship to the rest of the world has been constrained by a traditional colonial model: provider of a monocultural raw material (sugar, minerals) to the colonizer and consumer of manufactured materials from abroad.

U.S. Control and the Platt Amendment

Until its belated "independence" in 1902, this dependence was maintained under the gun of the Spanish crown. Between 1898 and 1902, following the Spanish-American War, Cuba was controlled by the United States military. Although nominal independence was achieved in 1902, it was granted by the United States only after Cuba had signed the 1901 Platt Amendment, which allowed for U.S. intervention in Cuba to protect American interests. The naval base at Guantánamo, established in 1903, was the first tangible result of the Platt Amendment, and today remains attached to Cuba like a tick to a deer, off-limits to Cubans.

Economic dependency precludes value-added products, those that receive industrial or intellectual elaboration prior to export. Only value-added products can create new local jobs and stimulate an export economy. But most of Cuba's raw materials went straight from the farm or mine to the docks.

Two decades after the Platt Amendment and following various U.S. interventions, U.S. companies owned a majority portion of Cuba's farmland and mines, and the Amendment, no longer needed, was abrogated in 1934.

Into the Soviet Circle

Whether the revolution of 1959 was communist from the outset or simply nationalist in the tradition of Cuban patriot José Martí is still argued among historians today. Whether Cuba drifted into the Soviet orbit by design or necessity, the result was three more decades of dependency on a foreign power. Economically benevolent as the Soviets may have been, they maintained Cuba as a monocultural supplier of sugar. Instead of allowing the economy to attain a certain degree of self-sufficiency, the Soviets seduced Cuba into receiving cheap products, including vital oil, in exchange for sugar, for which the Soviet bloc paid a premium price. Cuba's dependent agricultural technology was based on a classic, unsustainable model used by both the Soviets and North Americans.

Cuban agricultural scientists "express resentment toward Soviet and other socialist bloc advisers who were responsible for technology transfer to Cuba, and they were self-critical for having had a 'colonized mentality'," according to agrarian experts Peter Rosset and Medea Benjamin.

THE SPECIAL PERIOD

In effect, Cuba did not become truly independent until 1991, and by that time, a powerful globalized economy made it virtually impossible for any one small country to create its own local form of survival, although audacious Cuba strives to do just that today. With the collapse of Soviet support, the then three-decade U.S. economic embargo against Cuba was intensified, in expectation of the imminent fall of the Fidel Castro government.

The post-Soviet hardships suffered by Cubans are now legendary. But Cuba's health care and education systems, the best in all of Latin America, have remained functional, although reeling from the crisis.

This is the so-called "Special Period in a time of peace," with Cuba in the midst of reconstructing her economy in the absence of Soviet aid, while the United States tightens the embargo. The people have been asked to tolerate huge shortages of food, medicines, and fuel. During this period of "independence," Cuba has turned to tourism, "a necessary evil," and to courageous but risky experiments in organic agriculture to lift herself out of the Special Period. In the meantime, the 1992 Torriceli Act in the United States prohibited foreign subsidiaries of U.S. corporations from trading with Cuba and placed a six-month ban on ships that have docked at Cuban ports.

The 1996 Helms-Burton law allows U.S. investors to take legal action in U.S. courts against any foreign company that utilizes property in Cuba confiscated during the revolution.

National Pride

Throughout her history as a colony and neo-colony, Cuba was forced into the severe constraints of economic dependence on major world powers. Nationalist sentiment arising as a countercurrent to this dependency may explain why Cuba did not follow in the footsteps of Eastern European countries and accept the terms of the Western financial establishment. If there were ever a chance for Cuba to find her own wobbly path, it was in the 1990s, since she was now a satellite without a planet to revolve around.

Whether national pride can get this country through a period of extreme hardship is one of the main plots in the contemporary Cuban drama.

Guantanamera

During the height of the Special Period, one of Cuba's greatest filmmakers, Tomás Gutiérrez Alea (1928–1996), directed his final film, *Guantanamera*. As in his internationally-acclaimed *Fresa y Chocolate* (1994), in *Guantanamera*, Gutiérrez Alea and his co-director Juan Carlos Tabio deflect a potential tragedy by using the Cuban talent of mixing pathos with humor. The film is a poetic portrayal of Cuba's most difficult post-1959 historical period, scripted by the great Cuban writer Eliseo Diego. The film's title and lyrical chorus is derived from the classic *guajira* (country folk song), a traditional medium for mixing tragedy with improvised comedy.

Guantanamera is required viewing for anyone who wishes to see how Cubans cope, survive, and eventually emerge with a victory of the heart. Like *Fresa y Chocolate*, a poignant critique of a formal policy that ostracized homosexuals, *Guantanamera* is sharply critical of Cuban bureaucrats, in a most comical way. All the main characters of the Special Period make their appearance, especially the creative hustlers who sneak contraband bananas in a hearse and receive a commission for bringing travellers to a clandestine restaurant. There is a brief cameo for the *jineteras*, and sex and eroticism are presented as the primary escape from hardship. The issue of the schizophrenic double currency is highlighted when the government funeral bureaucrat, lacking dollars, is denied service in several public establishments.

The Black Market

One of the contradictions of Cuba in the 1990s is a thriving black market. Foreigners will be approached by young men who "remove" cigars or rejects from cigar factories as "fringe benefits" and resell them on the streets. Others will simply befriend tourists in the hope of a free meal. Relationships with Cubans are vulnerable to being tainted by the juxtaposition of two incompatible economies. Deeper human relationships are achieved when the visitor breaks out from the tourist mold and lets it be known that he or she has come to Cuba to live the daily life.

Responses

Today's youth of Cuba did not experience the pre-1959 Batista period and were too young during the pre-1991 Soviet period to recall the days of full employment and more comprehensive social protection. At the same time, they are too old to qualify for the subsidies enjoyed by children under eight years of age. Cuban youth are the most likely sector of the population to harbor cynical attitudes towards the Cuban socialist experiment during a time of hardship.

Committed revolutionaries are also vulnerable to the cynicism of the times. "Those less dedicated to the revolution have risen to a superior economic status through black market activities," says Dr. Jorge Crisosto, a Chilean doctor who does volunteer work in Cuba through Catholic Relief Services. "But the more militant revolutionaries, those who truly believe in socialism, neither receive dollars from abroad nor find it comfortable to participate in the underground economy, so it is they who suffer the most during the Special Period."

23

While receiving some privileges, even the Communist Party insiders are not protected from the tribulations of the people. Ricardo, a Bolivian journalist friend, investigated the much-commented-on food lines and found the wife of the Minister of Culture waiting in line like the rest of the people. According to anti-Castro journalist Andrés Oppenheimer, Politburo member Carlos Lage's mother was often seen standing in line for hours at her neighborhood bakery.

During times of hardship, some Cubans find solace in the fact that there was once a much greater gap between people of privilege and the majority. Most black Cubans cannot forget that before the 1959 revolution they were the victims of overt racism, and that today's Cuba, with all its faults, allows citizens of African origin the same chances as whites, as even the hypercritical Oppenheimer admits on pages 158–59 of *Castro's Final Hour*, his "obituary" on Cuban socialism.

But 95 percent of all Cuban exiles are white. With white Cubans more likely to receive dollars from abroad, there may be a racial component embedded in emerging social divisions. In an attempt to compensate for the inequalities of the dollar economy, the government is beginning to tax dollar earnings, while leaving Cuban peso earnings free of taxation.

COLONIALISM

At the outset of the Spanish colonial period in the early 1500s, native Americans who did not die in revolts were put to work on *encomiendas*, Spain's term for a landholding in which Indians received religious instruction in exchange for their labor. *Repartimientos,* another legal ploy to obtain free Indian labor, were permits granted by the crown to gather temporary labor forces for specific projects in mines, plantations, or public works. Those Indians who did not perish from overwork would succumb to imported diseases like smallpox. Whether a few descendents of these native Cubans survive today is an unresolved polemic.

In their place, African slaves were brought in. By the 1840s there were nearly half a million Africans on the island, the major portion being of Yoruba descent.

During the first century and a half of colonial rule, Cuba was besieged by pirates. Forts of stone masonry in Havana and other bays around the island were built to repel enemy attacks. Virtually abandoned by the mother country after gold reserves were exhausted, Cuba became a haven for smugglers and low-lifes. Tobacco production eluded colonial control until the establishment of a Spanish trade monopoly. But British occupation between 1862–63 opened the country to free trade.

Colonial society was dominated by a white planter class. New class divisions emerged when peninsular Spaniards gained privileges at the expense of resentful *criollos* (Spaniards born in the Americas). Beneath the creoles were the free blacks, with black slaves holding up the system from the bottom.

Slavery

Colonialism and slavery in Cuba lasted nearly four decades longer than in other Latin American countries. Some reformers, including Father Félix Varela, were advocating independence and the abolition of slavery since the early 1800s. But the 1823 U.S. Monroe Doctrine defended the rights of Spanish dominion over Cuba, since the United States was hardly interested in seeing a Cuban slave rebellion that might spread to its own doorstep.

The triumph of former slaves in Haiti and brutally crushed Cuban slave rebellions in the 1830s and 40s generated abolitionist sentiment, and the planter class feared that the last chapter of its dominion was unfolding. To preserve their status, many planters flirted with having Cuba annexed by the slaveholding South of the United States. In 1850, former Spanish general Narciso López led an insurgency in the name of annexation by the United States.

A defeated López became the first famous Cuban exile in Miami. He later returned with a new outfit of soldiers and was defeated once again and executed. With the British hindering Spanish slave trade and the Spaniards vowing to phase out slavery, Mexican Indians and Chinese workers were imported to cut sugar cane.

THE FIRST WAR OF INDEPENDENCE

In 1868, landowner Carlos Manuel de Céspedes launched an independence revolt. Although he freed his own slaves, he avoided abolitionist pronouncements in order to secure the support of the landed aristocracy. Like the later Cuban Revolution, this military movement surged forth from the Oriente, the eastern region of the island of Cuba. By 1869, the insurgents had produced a constitutional document declaring the slaves free, although they were to continue to work on the plantations for a salary. The Spanish colonial armies were backed by the United States.

When Céspedes lost his influence and later his life in an ambush by the Spaniards, Máximo Gómez, a black exile from Santo Domingo, and Antonio Maceo, a Cuban mulatto, continued the ill-fated movement. Most insurgents yielded in 1879 in exchange for amnesty.

Cuban hero General Antonio Maceo rejected the amnesty. Maceo had to deal with racial resentment and intrigues from white underlings. (I found an eloquent letter written by Maceo to the president of the independence movement in which he called for racial equality and threatened to go abroad if his protest was not heard.) By the third quarter of the nineteenth century many landowners found it cheaper to pay their workers and let them otherwise fend for themselves. Slavery was phased out and ultimately abolished by the Spaniards.

But a caste system had evolved in which most preferred government jobs were granted to the creoles, with Afro-Cubans restricted to agricultural employment. Another ill-fated independence insurrection began in 1879 and was repressed after a year. With slavery abolished

in 1880, a system of indentured servitude called *el patronato* continued for another six years until an 1886 royal decree declared it illegal.

The evolving sugar, mining, cattle, and tobacco industries in Cuba increasingly sought United States investment as the Spanish Crown remained intransigent with respect to any autonomous Cuban development.

José Martí

Cuba's most venerated national hero, José Martí, was the central figure in the escalating anti-colonial struggle. Martí spent his childhood in Spain. Upon his return to Cuba, he was shocked by the

27

inhumane treatment of black slaves. During the ill-fated first independence insurrection in 1869, Martí published the newspaper *La Patria Libre*. He was jailed with hard labor and then exiled for anti-Spanish political activity.

After the first war of independence had been squelched in 1878, Martí returned to Cuba with a law degree from Spain. In 1879 he was arrested again and deported as a subversive, ending up in New York after passing through Europe. In New York, he helped organize an educational center for black Cuban exiles.

In 1895, Martí, the Dominican Máximo Gómez and Antonio Maceo parlayed their efforts into a second war of independence. The objectives of Martí's Cuban Revolutionary Party were freedom from political and economic domination by any foreign power, be it Spain or the United States, equality among Cubans regardless of class or color, and establishment of democratic processes. Martí did not live to see the short-lived victory as he was killed in battle. He was an advocate of racial equality, and had he remained alive, some of the anti-racist measures that had to wait until the 1959 revolution would have been enacted earlier. Martí is also remembered as a poet and essayist.

Gómez and Maceo asked the Cubans to suspend all economic activity that might be advantageous to the royalists, in what resembled the Special Period of the 1990s. Maceo was killed in Pinar del Río, and Gómez's troops were isolated in the eastern region. Riots broke out in Havana, and the U.S. battleship *Maine* was apparently sent to protect American citizens.

SPANISH-AMERICAN WAR

The pretext for U.S. intervention in Cuba in 1898 was the explosion of the battleship *Maine*, in which 266 U.S. sailors died. The Spaniards called the explosion an accident, triggered by the ship's ammunition supplies, but the U.S. called it an act of war. Some Cuban historians hypothesize that some zealous Americans themselves might have blown up the Maine as a pretext to intervene.

A weakened Spain would have preferred to capitulate with honor but was obligated to enter a hopeless war. On San Juan Hill, near Santiago, the Spanish soldiers, outnumbered by seven to one, held off a horde of Teddy Roosevelt's rough riders. The daylong battle resulted in heavy casualties on both sides, with the Spaniards retreating. Spain eventually achieved its goal of surrender while minimizing casualties. Victory was quick for the United States, helped mainly by the fact that Cuban independence insurgents had already debilitated the Spanish royal army.

INDEPENDENCE

With Spanish surrender, the U.S. army should have handed over Cuba to victorious rebel leader General Calixto García. But García and most of his troops were black, so the U.S. decided to leave Spanish municipal governments intact. General García continued his war against the Spaniards.

The Cubans were not invited to the 1898 Paris peace treaty ceremony between the U.S. and Spain. Cuba was placed under U.S. occupation, and the U.S. army disbanded the largely black rebels. White Spaniards remained in positions of authority.

General Leonard Wood, a medical doctor, injected a measure of idealism into the U.S. intervention by helping to eradicate yellow fever. But with the 1901 Platt Amendment limiting Cuban self-determination, Cuban independence was constrained, and the country fell under the reins of corrupt intermediaries with discriminatory policies until 1959. The United States intervened with force to put down an anti-racist rebellion of former slaves in 1912 in the western province of Pinar del Río, in the wake of massive anti-discrimination protests at the other end of the country that were squelched by government repression.

The U.S. stock market crash of 1929 catalyzed an economic depression in Cuba, calling attention to the negative effects of a dependent economy. The crisis was mitigated during the U.S. "prohibition" period in the early 1930s, when Cuba became a haven for rum-drinking tourists, with prostitution and gambling emporiums burgeoning.

In 1930, the great African-American poet Langston Hughes visited Cuba in search of the roots of Afro-Cuban music. He met his counterpart, Cuban poet Nicolás Guillén. The two poets would later translate each other's work, and Hughes encouraged Guillén to highlight the rhythms of Afro-Cuban music in his poetry. Guillén became the stimulus of a revolutionary cultural awakening.

Political revolutions of the times were less inspiring. Street fighting erupted between the government led by Gerardo Machado and a throttled Cuban opposition calling for an independent economy. The revolution of 1933 forced Machado to flee from the island.

Batista

A sergeant in the Cuban army by the name of Fulgencio Batista piggy-backed onto the rebellion, which also included Ramón Grau San Martín, a socialist and anti-imperialist. Grau became revolutionary provisional president and immediately enacted labor reforms. Grau denounced the Platt Amendment, and the United States denied recognition to his government.

In control of military factions, Batista, instigated by U.S. ambassador Sumner Welles, forced Grau out of office in 1934. The United States immediately recognized a government headed by a Batista appointee. A subsequent Treaty of Reciprocity gave preferential treatment to United States exports in Cuba. Batista crushed a labor rebellion in 1935.

After a period of interim regimes, Batista faced Grau in a 1940 presidential election. The Cuban Communist Party (PCC) chose to support Batista over the more progressive Grau. (The PCC's later failure to support the Castro revolution was not an isolated ideological quirk.)

Had Batista allowed unrigged elections, opposition candidate Fidel Castro might have been elected, and Cuba's controversial history in the second half of the twentieth century would have taken a different path. Grau later won back the presidency, only to allow his regime to decay in corruption. Cuban election politics were typical of many Latin American countries, long on idealistic proclamations and short on honesty.

Dizzy Gillespie and Afro-Cuban Music.

A depressing political scenario failed to inhibit Cuban culture. Like Langston Hughes, the great bebop trumpeter Dizzy Gillespie was enchanted by Cuba's rich cultural textures. Jazz legend Gillespie became enthralled with Cuban music during the late 1940s and collaborated with Cuban bongo and conga drummer Luciano (Chano) Pozo in a symbiotic relationship that would influence both Cuban and U.S. music, by way of Cuba's West African heritage.

Chano, associated with a Nigerian sect, spoke no English but Gillespie got him to teach his bassist Al McKibbon and drummer Max Roach complex Cuban "layered" rhythms. The immediate result was a music called Cubop. Contemporary Latin jazz is still influenced by the Dizzy-Chano synergy.

Cuba's liberating cultural scene often contrasts with dictatorial politics. On March 10, 1952, three months before an election that Batista had no chance of winning, he took power in a bloodless coup. Working-class Cubans and peasants were excluded from economic prosperity during the Batista dictatorship, and protestors faced un-precedented repression.

Fidel Castro

An opposition figure during the Batista dictatorship was Fidel Castro, the son of sugar planters from eastern Cuba. Castro studied under the Jesuits and became a law student at the University of Havana. He graduated from law school in 1950, after having traveled abroad to participate in rebellious activities in Santo Domingo and Colombia. Had his pitching been a notch more effective, he might have found a career in professional baseball. As a post-coup candidate before aborted elections, Castro circulated a daring petition to depose the Batista government. Although the court ruled against the petition, one bold judge, Manuel Urrutia Lléo, did not comply with the majority. Castro would later reward him for his revolutionary stance.

American Tourists

The administration of Fulgencio Batista was burdened by corruption. Class and race distinctions divided the Cuban population, and illiteracy and unemployment made the island no different from other impoverished Latin American countries, except, as a playground for affluent American tourists, these contradictions were more blatant.

Wealthy and middle class Cubans were relatively well off, in stark contrast to the impoverished majority, many of them mulattos and blacks. Batista himself was too dark to be admitted to the Havana Yacht and Country Club and had to inaugurate his own country club.

U.S. crime syndicate influence in the pre-1959 Cuban tourism industry is legendary.

REVOLUTION

After making no headway politically and seeing a partner tortured to death, the Cuban opposition movement, which included Fidel Castro, staged the July 26, 1953 assault on the Moncada army barracks. As usual, the insurgency had begun in the Oriente region.

Of the 119 insurgents, 55 were later tortured to death. Castro's men fled to the mountains, but Fidel was captured. Strangely, he was put on trial in spite of orders to have him killed. The young lawyer's defense statement became his famous manifesto, "History Will Absolve Me." Castro was sentenced to 15 years.

In 1955, a Batista interested in improving his international reputation, liberated all political prisoners. Castro fled to Mexico while the movement he left behind was co-opted by the government.

On December 2, 1956, the persistent Castro landed at the shores of Cuba with about 80 companions, among them Ernesto "Che" Guevara, the Argentine doctor-adventurer. After initial setbacks, the guerrillas scored some successes in 1957, and Fidel Castro was portrayed as an idealist by Herbert Matthews in the *New York Times*.

Later in 1957, a suicidal attack on Havana's presidential palace, whose object was to assassinate Batista, met with failure. Anyone associated with the attack and who could be captured was executed by Batista's troops. The brash Castro would stop at nothing, and characteristically made bold moves against heavy odds. He and his brother Raúl established fronts in the Sierra Maestra, Radio Rebelde began its broadcasts, and general strikes provided urban support. But notably absent from the escalating rebellion was the Soviet-style Cuban Communist Party.

Without communist support, Fidel's 300 rebels seemed especially vulnerable, and Batista sent in 10,000 troops to the Sierra Maestra to once and for all liquidate the revolution. The Batista attack was repelled, arms captured, and with the support of the people, Castro had now gained the upper hand.

(Less than a decade later, Che Guevara would attempt a similar David versus Goliath insurgency, a strategy labeled *foquismo*, in Bolivia, but without the network of social support enjoyed by the Cuban rebels.)

Guevara and Camilo Cienfuegos set up new fronts, and the revolution retraced the path of the independence wars, pushing westward.

On New Year's eve, December 31, 1958, my friend Art and his wife were anchored in Havana on a honeymoon cruise, as the revolutionary forces advanced westward. After the midnight toasts, Batista made a New Year's resolution to abandon the country, along with 40 million dollars from the Cuban treasury. Fearing revolutionary violence, Art's cruise captain decided to turn away from Cuba, and to this very day, Art believes Fidel owes him a honeymoon.

Che and Camilo were the first to enter Havana on January 2, with the support of a general strike called for by Fidel Castro. Castro arrived in Havana six days later.

TURNING TOWARD THE SOVIETS

Ever since the arrival of the Spaniards, Cuba had been manipulated by foreign powers. Some historians believe that a bizarre, self-fulfilling prophesy, originating in the U.S. White House, pushed Fidel into the arms of the Soviets. Others say that Fidel had always been a Marxist, as he himself later declared.

Questions about Cuban history, following the 1959 overthrow of Batista, revolve around two issues. First are Cuba's experiments with utopian social reforms, some of them successful, others failed. Second is the conflict between Cuba and the United States, with historians divided as to who pushed who first.

Cuba vs the U.S.—Who Pushed Who?

Supporters of the Cuban "process" of social change say that the U.S. began the conflict. They dig back into a history of U.S. interventions epitomized by the Platt Amendment. They also argue that when Castro attempted to visit U.S. President Dwight D. Eisenhower, the American military hero purposely scheduled one of his famous golfing excursions in order to elude the bearded warrior. Vice-president Nixon, who was in the process of accusing everyone to the left of John Wayne of being a communist, made accusations to the effect that history would not absolve Castro, following a meeting with the Cuban leader at the White House.

Anti-Castro historians allege that Cuba pushed first, by enacting the first agrarian reform on May 17, 1959, expropriating U.S.-owned property, and failing to resolve the issue of indemnization.

As several interim presidents presided over Cuban agrarian reforms, with confiscations of companies like United Fruit, the C.I.A. and former Batista mafia cronies attempted to spur uprisings against

Love him or hate him, you can't deny that Fidel is one of the most important, audacious figures of the twentieth century.

Castro. The regime of John F. Kennedy and the C.I.A. attempted on numerous occasions to assassinate Castro by using mafia hit men, according to investigator and historian Seymour Hersh, but the would-be exploding cigars never went off in Castro's face. The Kennedy regime flirted with plans for a full-scale invasion of the island.

The besieged Comandante responded to U.S.-backed military threats by creating popular militia and purging the opposition. A mass exodus of Cuban technical experts and professionals to the United States exacerbated the expected economic upheavals that always come with revolutions. News of summary trials and executions of 500 former Batista collaborators and those attempting to overthrow the revolution left many foreign observers trying to decide if Fidel was an idealist, a Stalinist, or some combination of the two. Che Guevara justified the executions with an "us or them" morality.

Marxism had preached that a deposed ruling class will never peacefully allow a revolution to exist, and this axiom was behind the executions. (When Chile's elected socialist president Salvador Allende was overthrown in a violent 1973 coup, defenders of the executions would say "I told you so," but revolutionary humanists argued that "you could have locked them up without killing them.")

In June of 1960, the U.S. State Department urged U.S.-owned refineries to refuse to refine Soviet crude oil. Cuba responded by nationalizing the refineries.

In July of 1960, the United States suspended the Cuban sugar quota, effectively cutting off 80 percent of Cuban exports to the United States. Was this policy a reaction against increased Soviet influence or did it accomplish the opposite of its intention, obligating Cuba to look for a new Sugar Daddy? It looked much like a self-fulfilling prophesy when the Soviets stepped in to buy the sugar that was refused by the United States.

The suspension of the U.S. sugar quota was followed by Cuba's August 1960 nationalization of U.S. private investments. Were these nationalizations in the cards or had a cause-and-effect phenomenon kicked in?

In less than a month, the United States responded with the now internationally unpopular economic embargo, and the Cuban government responded with more nationalizations.

While this was all happening, the Comités para la Defensa de la Revolución (CDRs) were organized. Depending on your political philosophy, these committees were an example of participatory democracy with grass roots support for neighborhood health care and universal culture and education, or they were the eyes and ears of Big Brother, or both.

By early 1961, the United States had broken diplomatic relations with Cuba, soon followed by the C.I.A.-backed Bay of Pigs invasion at Playa Girón, which was defeated within 72 hours by the Cubans. (One planner of the Bay of Pigs invasion was E. Howard Hunt, who would later gain infamy by botching the Watergate burglary of Democratic Party headquarters that led to the downfall of president Richard Nixon. Nixon had opened commercial channels with the two greatest communist threats, the Soviet Union and China, but maintained the embargo against tiny Cuba.)

SOCIAL REFORMS

During the heady early years of the revolution, Cuba was able to lift the status of blacks and women. Prostitution became an unnecessary profession as movies like *Lucía* taught women's dignity and literacy campaigns wiped out illiteracy. Although many Cuban doctors had left the country, a nationwide effort to establish universal health care led eventually to Cuba's position as the Latin American country with the most equitable health care system.

Unlike other Latin American budgets, Cuban financial resources went directly to the needs of its people, and this was reflected

Fifth Avenue, the main thoroughfare in Miramar. Miramar was an exclusive neighborhood in Havana until the revolution. Now its mansions are divided up into apartments or used as embassies.

statistically with great achievements in culture, sports, and medicine. On the other hand, Cuba's increasing dependency on the Soviet Union created a scenario ripe for future economic crises.

Across the Gulf, in Mexico, the dominant PRI party was maintaining itself in power for seven decades with a party dictatorship. But by holding heavily-manipulated elections every six years, Mexico continued to qualify for trade with the United States. In the early 1960s, Fidel could have called for Mexican-style elections and won them easily. He chose not to.

From the beginning of the revolutionary experiment, the Cubans attempted to maintain a certain degree of independence from their Soviet benefactors. In September of 1961, for example, Cuba was the only Latin American country at the founding conference of the movement of nonaligned nations. Could Cuba be a part of the nonaligned camp and yet still function within the Soviet umbrella, or was there a split personality within the Cuban body politic?

By late 1961, Castro had declared that "I am a Marxist-Leninist, and I shall be one to the end of my life." Some historians believe that Fidel was simply a Cuban nationalist, pushed into the arms of the Soviets by U.S. Cold War politics. Others insist that he had always been a Marxist-Leninist. In the nationalist tradition of José Martí and Antonio Maceo, Fidel Castro may have drifted into the Soviet camp as the only perceived means to stand up to the giant to the north. His domineering, macho personality, more paternalistic than the typical Latin American *cacique*, gave him the audacity to pull it off.

In early 1962, the Organization of American States (OAS), dominated by the United States, launched the ill-fated Alliance for Progress as an alternative to socialism, and suspended Cuba's membership. Cuba responded with calls for all Latin American people to "rise up against imperialism."

In October of 1962, the "Cuban missile crisis" was resolved when the Soviets, without consulting the Cubans, agreed to withdraw the missiles from Cuban soil in exchange for a U.S. pledge to not invade Cuba.

The United States then resorted to diplomatic methods in an attempt to engulf the island. In July of 1964, the Organization of American States adopted mandatory sanctions against Cuba and required all members to sever diplomatic and trade relations with the Castro government. Although such measures tended to push Cuba ever closer to the Soviet bloc, Castro would later criticize the Soviets for their relations with Latin American oligarchies. One of those oligarchies defeated Che Guevara's 1967 military incursion in Bolivia. After being captured, Guevara was summarily executed by the Bolivian military.

LATIN AMERICAN SUPPORT

Support for Cuba eventually came from within Latin America. Mexico had immediately refused to comply with the OAS sanctions, and the Latin American arts and letters community continued to back the Cuban reforms, which included the 1968 nationalization of 55,000 small businesses.

In late 1969, the first of many volunteer contingents of what was called the Venceremos Brigade arrived from the United States to help with the sugar harvest. The story of the culture shock of idealistic middle class Americans cutting sugar cane and their adjustment to rural Cuba is told in Sandra Levinson's 1971 *Venceremos* (Simon & Schuster).

Many Latin American writers withdrew their support for the Cuban revolution when their Cuban colleague, poet Heberto Padilla, was arrested for activities against state security in 1971. Padilla was imprisoned for 39 days, ostracized, and later obligated to make a humiliating confession. He later went to Spain, criticizing the Castro regime for "a basic suspicion of all intellectuals." For Padilla's account of the episode, see his *La Mala Memoria* (Bad Memoires), published by Plaza and Janes in Spain in 1989.

The defection of foreign intellectuals following the Padilla incident did not include a cadre of supportive writers led by Nobel Prize winning Gabriel García Márquez, who has remained faithful to the Cuban revolution to this very day, standing beside Fidel during the 1998 visit of the Pope.

García Márquez is well aware that in 1997, on a scale of 1 to 10, Cuba ranked 0.9, beneath all Latin American countries in the categories of access to information and free pluralistic exercise of freedom of expression, according to the Third Ibero-American Forum on Communications. But it's not hard to understand why García Márquez would prefer a flawed Cuban system to the drug violence, political corruption, and ruthless human rights abuses in his native Colombia.

Curiously, many Latin American intellectuals, such as Pablo Ramos, former chancellor of Bolivia's national university in La Paz, who battle for freedom of expression in their own countries, continue to support the Cuban revolution. "To be poor in Cuba is to share the problem with everybody," Ramos told this reporter. "Nobody dies from lack of medical attention. To be poor in the rest of Latin America is to live with uncertainty, without access to medical care or quality education."

Ramos blames the United States trade embargo for many of Cuba's problems, and defending Cuba is his way of standing up against "an imposed economic doctrine from the north that has only brought suffering to our country."

U.S.–CUBA CONFLICT.

A billboard in Havana within view of the U.S. Interests Section offices, depicts a soldier shouting across the Caribbean to a threatening Uncle Sam: "Hey imperialists, we are absolutely not afraid of you."

For U.S. administrations, the existence of prisoners of conscience in Cuba is one of the excuses for maintaining the trade embargo and rejecting diplomatic relations. But Latin American intellectuals not so friendly to the Castro regime as Ramos, often question the moral standards of U.S. policy, citing the fact that far more repressive regimes in their own countries have received U.S. blessing and support.

Anti-Castro extremists in the U.S. have been tolerated by the FBI. In October of 1976, a bomb was planted on a Cuban airliner, killing 73 people. Luis Posada Carriles, a Cuban exile and former C.I.A. employee, was arrested in Venezuela and charged with the bombing. Cuba responded by suspending its 1973 anti-hijacking accord with the United States. Cubans allege that the bomber today "walks free on the streets of Miami." After a rash of 1997 bombings of hotels and restaurants in Cuba, an obvious attempt to disrupt the tourist industry, Cuban exile leader Francisco Hernández declared: "we don't consider these actions terrorism, because people fighting for liberty cannot be limited by a system that is itself terrorist."

Geopolitical analysts explain that Cold War politics were behind the U.S. embargo of Cuba, since Cuba was in the Soviet camp. But in 1991, after a total divorce between Cuba and the Russians (Aeroflot doesn't even fly to Cuba anymore), the United States stiffened its trade restrictions against Cuba's economy. The 1996 Helms-Burton law was signed by a reluctant President Clinton after Cuba shot down two planes piloted by Hermanos al Rescate, an organization of Miami exiles. Whether or not the planes were illegally buzzing Cuban air space is a political rather than geographical opinion.

Helms-Burton allows U.S. investors to take legal action in U.S. courts against foreign companies utilizing their confiscated property in Cuba. It also prevents the lifting of the trade embargo until the Castro government no longer presides over Cuba, and requires U.S. representatives to international financial organizations to oppose loans to Cuba.

There is an ultimate cultural irony to the U.S.–Cuba conflict. Most Soviets who lived and worked in Cuba hardly integrated with the Cuban population, rarely learning Spanish and confining themselves to educational and social enclaves. The Soviets never overcame Culture Shock Cuba, and generally failed to partake in the joyful Caribbean culture. People from the United States, on the other hand, have many cultural affinities with Cuba, from Hemingway to baseball to Latin jazz.

From a cultural standpoint, Cuba's relationship with the Russians was a total flop, and her estrangement with the United States has been a tragic divorce between neighbors who would have gotten along fabulously.

INTERNAL MEASURES

During the revolutionary ferment of the 1960s, the concept of banking, a dominant aspect in most cultures, was considered of less moral virtue than cinema or sports. How could Che Guevara, an adventurer, a doctor, and a motorcyclist, be named the president of Cuba's National Bank?

Guevara expected his bank employees to increase productivity through moral rather than monetary incentives. Cuba's economic system was supposed to function through a cultural transformation. Guevara wanted to create *el hombre nuevo*, a new human being guided by moral values rather than materialism. He and his cohorts assumed that an idealist culture would generate productive forces better than one based on greed.

The banning of self-employment and the nationalization of small businesses in the late 1960s presumed that small enterprises fomented the same cultural maladies of exploitation and greed as larger enterprises and corporations. This unsuccessful policy was reversed 30 years later, and small business is today an important tax-paying sector of the economy.

In the late 1990s, rigid state controls were established to prevent a wealthy commercial class from rising above the rest, as Cuba gropes for methods to expand its economy evenly, without causing gaps in social and economic class. The monocultural dependency through sugar production and the near exclusivity of trade with the Soviet bloc was less an error and more an obligation of circumstances. This policy severely distorted Cuba's productive forces. Several attempts were made to diversify the economy, only to be abandoned in the throes of crisis situations that demanded escalation of sugar production.

A typical exchange with a disgruntled Cuban: "It's time for Fidel to step down. What we need is another Che." Che Guevara attempted to forge an economy based on moral rather than material incentives. He called this cultural transformation El Hombre Nuevo (the New Man). He did not live long enough, however, to follow through on his program.

These are but a few of the errors now openly recognized by most Cubans, including members of the governing party. But in spite of these errors, the quality of life at the bottom end of Cuban society was notably better than that of poor people in the rest of Latin America, in the realms of health, education, and culture.

43

"In fact," writes skeptic Oppenheimer, "some of the government's claims were legitimate, even if exaggerated. That was why many Cubans were still finding positive aspects in a revolution that was otherwise marked by economic failure."

"It was true that in the Cuba of the late 1980s you didn't find the pockets of misery you stumbled on in virtually any other Latin American country," wrote Oppenheimer, whose book against Castro was banned in Cuba but widely read anyway. "There were no beggars on the streets—at least no full-time ones ... Cuba had eliminated misery at the cost of imposing a general poverty."

Will Cuban utopian attempts to forge a new, non-materialist culture eventually succumb to what critics call human nature?

TEÓFILO STEVENSON

The more politicized Cuban ideologues seemed demagogic in their sloganeering, as if they were posturing to satisfy their Soviet backers. But Cuba's greatest all-time heavyweight boxer, Teófilo Stevenson expressed the ideas of the *hombre nuevo* by his actions.

Stevenson, along with runner Alberto Juantorena and javelinist María Colón represented Cuba's first generation of Olympic champions. In Montreal in 1976, Juantorena broke the record for the 800 meters and then went on to win the 400 meters, the first man to take both events in the Olympics. Also in Montreal, María Colón became the first third-world athlete to win a gold medal in women's athletics, at the same time that back in Cuba, women's literacy was equaling that of men, also an unprecedented achievement for a third-world country.

Heavyweight boxer Teófilo Stevenson would face his greatest decision out of the ring. In 1972 in Munich, they called Stevenson "the most impressive Olympic boxer since Cassius Clay." The United States' Duane Bobick had defeated Stevenson in the previous Pan American Games. But Stevenson went home to work on his right hand to accompany his stinging left jab. Bobick went into the rematch unconcerned. But the improving Stevenson battered the American and the fight was stopped in the third round. Germany's Peter Hussing was also knocked out by Stevenson. "I have never been hit so hard in all my 212 bouts," said the seasoned Hussing.

After Stevenson's first gold medal, fight promoters were after him. They wanted him to fight Mohammed Ali for the heavyweight championship. Stevenson responded that he was more interested in his studies and in the revolution than in making a million dollars. So they offered him two million.

"Professional boxing treats a fighter like a commodity to be bought and sold and discarded when he is no longer of use," responded Stevenson. "Mohammed Ali makes millions, but he's exploited nonetheless."

In the 1976 Olympics, Teófilo Stevenson knocked out his first three opponents in a record 7 minutes and 22 seconds. His last opponent was the Romanian Mircea Simon, who dodged Stevenson completely for the first two rounds. When Stevenson finally hit his opponent in the third round, Simon's seconds immediately threw in the towel. Simon defected to the United States. Stevenson went back to Cuba.

In 1980, in Moscow, a slower Stevenson became the first boxer to win three Olympic gold medals in the same division.

LIVÁN HERNÁNDEZ

A more recent case of a star athlete offered millions to defect is baseball pitcher Liván Hernández. Cuba has no celebrity industry, and an athlete who excels like Liván is going to end up teaching Physical Education with only a few extra perks like the use of a house, a car and travel expenses abroad. But Hernández's skills were worth millions of dollars in the global economy. Hernández became the four-million-dollar man and led his Miami team to a world series baseball championship in 1997.

In Cuba, Hernández's name was banned from all media. His half brother, Orlando "El Duque" Hernández, older and perhaps even better than Liván, fell under uncorroborated suspicion that he had helped Liván escape. El Duque, a national hero, was banned from Cuban baseball.

The irony was that El Duque Hernández, a committed communist in the tradition of Teófilo Stevenson, had been subjected to repeated aggressive recruiting whenever playing abroad and had always refused millions to defect. Once ostracized, El Duque depended on Liván's gifts from abroad to supplement his income as a physical therapist. But a further irony is that El Duque rarely received economic help from his wealthy brother abroad.

In ruining El Duque's career at home, the Cuban bureaucracy scored points in either incompetence, paranoid behavior, or both. It was not the first time that a zealous bureaucrat had given a bad name to the very system he was supposedly defending. A committed socialist and ideal sports ambassador for the Cuban system, El Duque himself was obligated to flee, and in his case, he did not do it for the money.

"Surely you must understand the motives of guys like Liván Hernández," I argued to a faithful Cuban party member. "Not every star should be expected to resist like Teófilo."

Off the record, he went beyond the official discourse:

"We understand what Liván did," he said. "But what we don't understand is the way he did. He could have arranged to go there and send back half his salary to contribute to the education of his countrymen, like other Cubans do who go abroad. Liván has a contract for four and a half million! Does any human being need that much?"

Given the enormous financial incentives, it is amazing that so many Cuban baseball heroes have refused to defect. When star infielder Omar Linares was under intense pressure during the 1996 Atlanta Olympics to remain in the United States and play for the New York Yankees, he responded:

"I'd rather play for 11 million Cubans than 11 million dollars."

FOREIGN ADVENTURES

Many Cubans are today critical of Cuba's militant involvement in affairs on other continents. Cuba's defense of Angola against South African mercenaries, although temporarily successful, led to a loss of lives of many Cuban soldiers, the best trained in all of Latin America. This excursion in Angola against South Africa's racist regime won Cuba favor amongst the nonaligned nations, a group that represented an alternative to Soviet dominance. In 1984, Cuba agreed to withdraw from Angola in exchange for the removal of South African troops from Namibia. But when Cuba sent troops to Ethiopia, entering a sectarian squabble between two communist factions, it did so to satisfy the demands of the Soviet Union. This was one of several policies that prevented the reopening of diplomatic relations between Cuba and a receptive U.S. president , Jimmy Carter.

After the October 22 assassination of Grenadan socialist Prime Minister Maurice Bishop, Cuba denied a request from the Grenadan coup leaders to assist the island country against an impending U.S. invasion. Three days later, 8,800 U.S. troops invaded Grenada, where 734 Cubans were on the island at the bequest of the murdered Bishop to construct an airport. Only 43 of the Cubans were military personnel. U.S. forces captured 642 Cubans, killing 24 and wounding 57.

HUMAN RIGHTS

In 1987, the United States sponsored a U.N. resolution harshly criticizing Cuba for alleged human rights violations. The resolution was voted down by the U.N. Human Rights Commission and only one of eight Latin American representatives on the commission voted with the United States.

In 1988, a delegation of U.S. human rights leaders inspected Cuban prisons, in exchange for a subsequent visit of a Cuban delegation to U.S. prisons. The U.S. group reported that "conditions in Cuban prisons were generally no worse than those in U.S. prisons" and that there was no evidence of systematic abuses. The U.S. group also concluded that some prison policies in Cuba, such as conjugal visits, are more humane than those in the United States.

According to the 1997 Amnesty International report, in 1996 one Cuban was the victim of a political execution and there were approximately 800 prisoners of conscience or political prisoners on the island. On the other hand, Cuba has not been riddled by death squads a la El Salvador, Guatemala, and Honduras, nor have protesters been massacred, as has happened often in Mexico between 1968 and 1997, nor does rampant torture exist as it did in Argentina and Chile.

If human rights have to do with the rights of children to a good education and to universal health care, one Cuban diplomat argued to this writer, then no other country in Latin America can rival Cuba's success.

Personally, as a writer, I would not feel comfortable within Cuban press restrictions, which allow for "everything within the revolution but nothing outside of it." I raised this issue with a Cuban official. He responded that the person on the street in Cuba, with neighborhood committees and forums, has much more of a chance to make his expression effective than his counterpart in countries where there is an all-powerful corporate media, and where if you don't have the money to own a newspaper, you have no say.

Prior to the Pope's visit to Cuba in January 1998, the Vatican had presented the Cuban government with a list of 270 prisoners it wanted released. Within weeks of the Pope's departure, more than 300 prisoners were released, and for the first time, the Cuban government recognized that political prisoners existed. Such inmates had previously been labeled as common criminals. But in a follow-up article in *Granma*, Castro warned that the release of prisoners should not be construed as a softening of Cuba's political position.

"The Cuban regime would offer greater evidence of change," said a member of the Latin American Association of Human Rights in a February 1998 Reuters article, "if the government of the United States would put an end to the illicit blockade, which violates the fundamental principles of human rights."

FREEDOM OF MOVEMENT

The history of emigration from Cuba since 1959 involves numerous examples of apparent limitations on freedom. The most contemporary phenomenon is the so-called "Palestinians," rural Cubans who emigrate to the city. When shantytowns of "Palestinians" began appearing in pockets of Havana, the government clamped down and prohibited migration from rural areas to the capital.

I asked a Cuban diplomat why it was that so many Cubans leave their country. Typical of Cuban officials, even when presenting ideas that are obviously in accord with government policy, he asked that his name be withheld. "There are more Bolivians outside of Bolivia," he responded, "than Cubans who've left Cuba. The whole Cuban population that has left the country is equivalent to the number of Mexicans who leave Mexico in one month."

"The problem is economic," he continued. "In fact, more than any other national group, Cubans are lured to the United States because they receive a special welcome there, with social benefits."

A chronology of Cuban emigration since the revolution begins in the years between 1959 and 1962, when any Cubans who wanted to leave could simply hop on a daily flight to Miami, with the condition that they leave behind everything owned. In the second half of the 1960s, the U.S. government automatically declared all Cuban immigrants to be eligible for residency, a dream always denied to Mexican neighbors. A quarter of a million Cubans took advantage of the offer.

In 1980, a totally different wave of emigrants, the *marielitos*, of humbler origins, were allowed to leave Cuba. A crafty Fidel used the crisis to dump convicted prisoners and the mentally ill on the United States. The crisis began when 7,000 Cubans were allowed to seek asylum in the Peruvian embassy in Havana. By 1984, the ever-creative Castro found a new tactic. Former political prisoners and their families were allowed to flee the island, thus ridding the system of its most vociferous dissenters. The 1996 Amnesty International report expresses concern over Cuba's recurring to exile as a form of ridding herself of internal opposition.

50

In the early 1990s, in the wake of a youth riot, Castro allowed the *balseros* (emigrants in make-shift rafts) the right to navigate to Florida, with President Clinton opening the doors at the other side. Immediately following the Soviet collapse, Cubans had been subjected to intense hardships, and many felt they had nothing to lose. Many never made it through the shark-infested waters. Clinton eventually rescinded the invitation, and the *balseros* were picked up at sea and taken to Guantánamo Naval Base. Most of them ended up in the United States anyway.

Although anti-Castro activists say such migrations have been political, most Cuban emigration seems mainly economic in origin. The *balseros* rightfully received the sympathy of many people in the United States, although ironically, the U.S. blockade was at least partially responsible for the economic asphyxiation that led to their flight.

In a larger context, illegal immigrants from Mexico and Central America, whose economic situation has been even more desperate than that of the *balseros*, since they enjoy no social protection, choose to risk death by dehydration and set out to cross the Arizona and California deserts or suffocate in truck trailers while trying to make it to Los Angeles. Those who arrive are not welcomed like Cubans, and are considered an alien enemy by media-driven public opinion within the United States.

THE SPECIAL PERIOD IN A TIME OF PEACE

Communism collapsed, the U.S. embargo stiffened, and Cuba confronted ominous food, fuel, and medical shortages. Eastern Europe caved in and hoped that primitive capitalism would solve its crisis. Grotesque social inequalities and a rise in organized crime left many Eastern European countries in economic purgatory. Eastern Europeans found it easy to discard an economic system that was imposed from abroad.

But in the face of a U.S. "blockade," for Fidel Castro to give in would be nothing less than total surrender, hardly in keeping with the tradition of José Martí. Castro decided to defend Cuba's socialist experiment. This means an extended period of drastic penance during which many of the people who once loved Fidel would learn to hate him.

To counteract fuel shortages, Cubans were given new bicycles, and Castro, sounding like fellow authoritarian and idealist Don Quixote, said that this would be good for Cubans' health and the country's ecology. Castro pointed to Holland, where the use of automobiles is discouraged and the bicycle is lauded. Oxen replaced gas guzzling tractors, and urban dwellers were encouraged to make trips to the country to resolve the food shortage by planting and harvesting. Many refused, but many more went back to the land and in typical Cuban style, found a way to party while doing so.

Tourism has been expected to bail out the country, but the clumsy relationship between the new dollar economy and the Cuban peso created new divisions in social class. Laws permitting self-employment and small private business suddenly made many new products available. Can a flawed but egalitarian Cuba survive?

Many Cuban insiders are not pleased with the results of the dual dollar-peso economy and resulting social inequities. Long-time-insider Ricardo Alarcón, president of the National Assembly of People's Power, was remarkably frank to the foreign press during the Pope's visit:

"While it is true that we have some things in our reality that are not to our liking—the dual economy, the circulation of dollars—," he said, "that was done out of necessity. But it is something that we should try to eliminate, the sooner, the better."

DRAMATIC TIMES

At the outset of the decade, investigators like Andrés Oppenheimer gloated over the hardships of the Special Period, and predicted the imminent downfall of Fidel Castro. But by 1997, with a growing economy, Castro had outlived the dire predictions, and the January

1998 visit of the Pope injected new energy into the Cuban system. The Pope criticized the existence of political prisoners within Cuba, but he also lashed out at the U.S. trade embargo.

Less certain was what would happen to the bedrock of revolutionary Cuba, the health care system, universal education, a high level of culture, and what remained of social equality. Only this modicum of equality, as well as a thriving underground economy, prevents disaffected, dollarless youth from breaking out in violent acts of rebellion.

Foreign tourism entrepreneurs have been allowed to recover their initial investments before sharing their profits with the Cuban public, which means that expected benefits from tourism had not yet kicked into full force by the time of the Pope's visit in 1998.

Even the most cynical Cubans I interviewed testified that by 1997, things were much better. The image of Fidel Castro is now tarnished among a large sector of youth, but this does not mean that they want Miami exiles to control their fate. A new phenomenon involves socialist exiles who leave the country because of tourist-related social inequities, adding further complications to an already convoluted social scenario.

"Do the people criticize Castro," asked many anxious Americans.

"Yes they do," I answered. On every street corner you hear them. But one of the typical codas to an anti-Fidel sonata is: "We need someone like Che," hardly the response that the Miami exile elite wants to hear. The question remains whether the government can juggle two diametrically-opposed tiers of the economy, using doses of capitalism to save socialism.

"Why not embrace full-fledged capitalism at once?" wrote Andrés Oppenheimer. "In the minds of a growing number of Cubans, cold-blooded capitalism would make more sense than well-meaning socialism with dwindling social programs."

Not so, according to Adam Kufeld, whose three trips to Cuba extended over a two-year period and ended during the most difficult phase of economic crisis. Back in 1994, he wrote: "Many are frustrated with the authoritarianism and the intolerance of political dissent," but "hardly anyone thinks capitalism is the answer" when they see the sobering reality of the market economy on neighboring island countries of Haiti, Jamaica, the Dominican Republic, and Puerto Rico."

"I think the future belongs to democracy," said Ricardo Alarcón, "but not to capitalism, because they are opposite camps. We believe the government has to intervene precisely for the benefit of those who would be deprived if you leave democracy to the market."

In the meantime, Cuban culture continues to enthrall virtually everyone who dares to visit the island. The Cuban way of life, independent of economic systems and political discourse, is highly contagious, to everyone, it seems, but the Soviets who remained here in their enclaves.

The rest of this book will explore the seductive Cuban culture.

Chapter Two

PHYSICAL SETTING

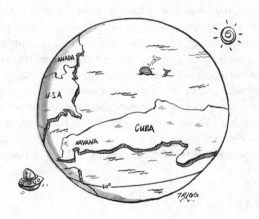

CULTURE AND CLIMATE

Mainland Cuba is a tropical island in Latin America. In general, Latin Americans from tropical regions tend to be more spontaneous and exuberant than those from cooler highlands. Just how much of the Cuban spontaneity comes from her tropical heritage and how much is uniquely Cuban?

I have traveled for two decades in search of an answer to this enigma, through other tropical habitats such as Veracruz, Mexico, El Salvador, Costa Rica, Panamá, and Ecuador. My subjective impression is that frankness and spontaneity among Cubans, or between Cubans and foreigners, is yet more prominent than in other regions of the tropics. Tropical Caribbean stereotypes are only partially applicable to Cuba.

Anthropologists still debate the effect that setting has on character. Many Cubans I've interviewed sincerely believe that their Miami brothers and sisters have lost some of the collective spark (*la chispa*) by having been subjected to a way of life that trades in community values for stressful consumerism.

Cubans on their native turf have no choice but to get along with each other, cramped as they are in the odd camel buses (*camellos*), two-humped windowed trailers hauled by diesel truck cabins. Back in Miami, Florida, air conditioning, elaborate home entertainment products, and an automobile lifestyle, leave most streets empty. In Cuba, small apartments with no air conditioning encourage people to occupy the street, the park, or the Malecón, the long seawall in Havana, which all become the neighborhood living room.

Without discerning more precisely which aspects of setting have greater or lesser impact on the culture, let's take a glimpse at Cuba's physical setting.

GEOGRAPHY

Most of Cuba is one island 1,250 kilometers (777 miles) long (west–east) but only 191 kilometers (119 miles) wide (north–south) at its widest section. The island is like a misshapen fish, 160 kilometers (100 miles) southwest of the Florida Keys and 210 kilometers (130 miles) east of Mexico's Yucatán peninsula.

But the Republic of Cuba is more than an island. It is 1,600 islands, islets, and keys: an archipelago. It is a haven for a yachtsman with time to explore. The second largest piece of real estate on the archipelago is Isla de la Juventud, a sparsely populated beach paradise. Cuba's 6,073 kilometers (3,770 miles) of coastline include bays with narrow entrances that open out into great harbors, rugged cliffs, coral reefs, and various swamplands.

North and east of Cuba lies the Atlantic Ocean. To her west is the Gulf of Mexico. To her south is the Caribbean Sea. Cuba is the fifteenth largest island in the world. One fourth of her surface is

Valley of Viñales, famous for tobacco growing and the flat-top mountains called mogotes.

forested mountains. The rest is comprised of fertile plains, somewhat depleted by chemical agriculture, but now being restored with an ambitious plan for organic agriculture. Sugar cane, cattle, tobacco, rice, and coffee are Cuba's most traditional crops. Citrus fruits are making a comeback after a failed experiment to convert Cuba into a dairy economy. Colonial and neocolonial powers have used Cuba's land to produce non-nutritional farm products: sugar, tobacco, coffee, and rum. Cuba's land has traditionally yielded a myriad of after-dinner delights without setting aside enough of its acreage for the main course.

Mountain Ranges

The main island is not known for its mountains, but three attractive ranges, referred to as *alturas*, look down on its green plains and valleys. The Cordillera de Guaniguanico, in the western province of Pinar del Río, reaches its highest point with El Pan de Guajaibón at 692 meters (2,270 feet).

Continuing from left to right, we find the second range, the Sierra de Escambray, in the southern part of Cuba's central provinces of Cienfuegos and Sancti Spíritus. The highest peak in this range is San Juan, also called La Cuca, at 1,156 meters (3,793 feet).

Continuing eastward, the third and most fabled range, near the southeast coast just west of Guantánamo Bay, is the Sierra Maestra, which sheltered the revolutionary forces of Fidel Castro between 1956 and 1959. The highest peak here, climbable in six hours and with a breathtaking view, is Pico Real del Turquino, at 1,974 meters (6,476 feet), high enough for a refreshing change in climate.

With most of Cuba's population density in the environs of Havana, many nooks and crannies, including pristine beaches and unexplored coves, await the meditative sojourner. For at least another few years, Cuba will remain one of the least commercialized paradises in the world, with none of the drug problems that plague other Latin American and Caribbean regions. Nature lovers can delight in fishing, hiking, scuba diving, bird watching, and cross-country bicycle trips.

Rivers

The majority of Cuba's more than 500 watercourses are short and skimpy with water, but may rise to the occasion during the rainy season. Cuba's largest rivers are found in the southeast, where the 370-kilometer (230 mile) Río Cauto springs out of the Sierra Maestra above Santiago and travels northeast, emptying out into the Gulf of Guacanayabo.

Climate

Cuba lies in what is considered a torrid zone at the northern edge of the tropics, although one rarely feels such notorious extremes in heat of summers as in U.S. or southern European cities. Trade winds of northerly origin temper the extremes that would be found in other tropical regions at the same latitude of the Tropic of Cancer.

The annual mean temperature, for example, is only 26°C (79°F). This average dips to 23°C (73°F) in January, the coolest month, and rises to no more than 28°C (82°F) in August, the hottest month, in mid-summer vacation. During a normal year, Cuba's high temperature is only 32°C (90°F). For comparison's sake, consider that there is never a summer in Washington D.C. that doesn't see the mercury hit at least 37°C (99°F), with equally high humidity as Cuba. (Humidity averages about 80 percent.) The lowest possible temperature during a normal year will be 16°C (61°F).

If the weather has a say in determining your travel to Cuba, bear in mind that the heart of the rainy season extends from May through October, and the hurricane season runs from June through November, although September and October are the most likely months for a hurricane. Cuba is pleasantly mild from late-October through March.

Living Things

Ever since colonial times, Cuba has been victimized by deforestation. Her three mountain ranges have acted as fortresses against the total decimation of her forests. One day I will discover why, in so many countries in Latin America, reforestation primarily involves eucalyptus trees not native to the region.

As might be expected, the palm tree is Cuba's most characteristic sight, with the royal palm on the country's coat of arms. The unusual big belly palms appear as if they are pregnant. My favorite Cuban tree is the multi-trunked *jaguey*, whose shade is more refreshing than that of any other tree I've known. Although the *jaguey* is kind to human beings in this respect, it kills every plant around it, so bring a blanket if you do not wish to sit in the dirt under this tree.

Other trees are the silk-cotton tree (wide trunk, swelling at the top), and big-leaf trees like the banana tree and *yagruma*. I've spotted *agaves* in dry areas, the same century plants used in Mexico to make tequila.

Orchid lovers will be pleased by Cuba's numerous species. My favorite flower, because of its aroma, is the jasmine. The *mariposa,* or butterfly jasmine, is Cuba's national flower. More than 3,000 surviving species of plants are native to Cuba, and several thousand others have been imported to the island during different historical periods.

In order to appreciate Cuba's animal life, you'll have to get beyond her developed tourist regions. Public transportation is sparse to the offshore islands, the mountains, and the swamps of Ciénega de Zapata, so consider hiring a yacht to the islands, hiking or cycling from the nearest town to the mountains or swamps, or taking an ecotour.

The animal kingdom in Havana lacks what is so prominent in other Latin American capitals: stray dogs. Shortages in red meat and food in general or a hyperefficient public health system may partially explain the virtual absence of strays in many neighborhoods.

There are a few notable surviving wilderness animals. In the Ciénega de Zapata resides a living fossil called the alligator gar (*manjuarí*), part fish and part reptile. Even more difficult to find is a nocturnal snake in the python family called *majá*, who won't dare visit your hotel room or backyard garden.

A large bat population performs its social function, going on nightly hunting forays and thereby preventing mosquitos from bothering Cuba's human population. Other rare beings include the manatee, a living sea fossil, and the *jutía*, a mammal nicknamed "tree rat" that is rarely found in populated areas. Cuba is not an ideal place for lovers of wild animals.

Melania, a gourmet cook, cringes at the thought of eating the *jutía* "because it looks like a big rat," but her husband Nufo says it tastes fine. Melania prefers the meat of the *majá* snake.

Bird watchers will have a better opportunity to observe unusual species. Start with Cuba's national bird from the quetzal family, the *tocororo*, easy to pick out with its red, white, and blue feathers that match the Cuban flag. Among Cuba's 350 bird species is the world's smallest bird, the bee hummingbird (*pájaro mosca*), but Cuba's urban development has exiled this rare bird to the Ciénega de Zapata.

My favorite Cuban bird, because of its streamlined beauty, its "social" function, and its willingness to pose for pictures, is the white cattle egret, called *garza*. It seems as if one egret has been assigned to each cow by the government bureaucracy. The egret devours evil parasitic insects called *garrapatas* from the cow's hide.

Perhaps Cuba's greatest hero in the animal kingdom is a parasitic fly called the *Lixophaga diatraeae,* big name for a small guy who devours the deadly sugar cane borer and thereby saves Cuba's foreign exchange.

REGIONS WEST TO EAST

Regions in Cuba should be called slices. Cuba is shaped like a long sea animal with the mouth to the left (west) and the fins to the right (east). Regions are divided by north-south slices. Moving from left/west to right/east, below is an annotated list of Cuba's regions or provinces.

Cultural center in town of Viñales, province of Pinar del Río. With scarce resources, Cuba went against conventional Latin American wisdom and invested heavily in rural regions, while leaving colonial city streets in disrepair.

61

Pinar del Río

This province, whose capital city of the same name has a population of less than 150,000, is the core of Cuba's tobacco region. Tobacco fields are presided over by the *mogotes*, flat-top limestone mountains that resemble the peculiar outcrops in Quilin in southern China. Throughout the area, around the immaculate, pinetree town of Viñales, are remarkable cave labyrinths, carved out by rivers and waterfalls.

Resorts are scattered throughout the lush green, mountainous province. Bird watching, swimming, fishing, scuba diving, ecotourism, and visits to cigar factories are a few of the activities available to visitors.

Province of Havana

The City of Havana is Cuba's main attraction, while the province of Havana remains a well-kept secret. It is often easier to find transportation to more distant regions than to places right around Havana, like San Antonio de los Baños, famous for its school of cinema and its Museum of Humor.

The City of Havana has been exempted from the contradictions of every other major city in Latin America. Architect Miguel Coyula, of the Group for the Integral Development of the City of Havana, explains why. "It is a city that hasn't been touched by the second half of the twentieth century because efforts of renovation have been focused on rural Cuba, in order to correct the tremendous imbalance between country and city so typical of Latin America."

The emphasis on rural development spared Havana from the anarchic waves of rural-to-urban immigration so typical in Latin America, and averted the spawning of a rural-rooted urban underclass that has bred social violence in cities like Caracas, Lima, and Mexico City.

Since Havana originated in the east and spread west, a walker can time travel through the historical periods of the city, beginning in colonial Old Havana, with each subsequent sector representing the next historical style of architecture. Along the way are baroque, rococo, art nouveau, and art deco buildings. One begins on narrow

Vedado neighborhood of Havana. Old cars are so common that they've become a part of Cuba's psychic geography.

streets lined with ornate facades and balconies. Walking farther west, the streets become wider, the green areas larger, and the styles of buildings and homes more modern.

"Old Havana is the only colonial city in Latin America with a totally intact infrastructure," explains architect Coyula with glee. "That's because there was no land speculation there."

Beyond the city, good beaches with few tourists (try Playa Jibacoa, with an unusual limestone ridge, 60 kilometers [37 miles] east of the city) and organic agricultural communities struggling to feed the city make for interesting visits if you can rustle up a ride out of town.

Matanzas

The capital, of the same name, is about the size of Pinar del Río. This province is mainly known for the resorts in Varadero and the historic Bay of Pigs, now a favored spot for scuba divers. Many Cubans find Varadero offensive, as it is off limits to them economically. My daughter went there anyway and found the underground beach-dune economy fascinating. But she preferred Playa del Este to the east of Havana.

Villa Clara and Cienfuegos

Villa Clara (north) and Cienfuegos (south) share the same slice of central Cuba. Villa Clara's capital, Santa Clara, approaching a quarter of a million inhabitants, has typical Cuban *ambiente* but without significant numbers of tourists. Songs about Che Guevara feature Santa Clara, the site of Che's historic 1958 military victory that led to the downfall of Batista. One can cool off in picturesque mountains south of the city, part of the Sierra de Escambray. Remedios, one of Cuba's more original colonial towns, with some structures dating back to the 1500s, is northeast of the city of Santa Clara.

The bay city of Cienfuegos (about the size of Pinar del Río and Matanzas), is a large industrial center. The province of the same name is probably the least African of all Cuban regions. It shares the Escambray mountains with both Villa Clara and Sancti Spíritus.

Sancti Spíritus

The city of Sancti Spíritus is rather small for a provincial capital, with less than 100,000 inhabitants. Within the province of Sancti Spíritus is also the colonial city of Trinidad with 50,000 inhabitants, declared a World Heritage Site by UNESCO. If you had to choose one baroque place to visit during a trip to Cuba, this might be it. It's about 450 kilometers (280 miles) from Havana, a six-hour ride. Also in Sancti Spíritus is the highest mountain of the Escambray range, Pico San Juan (La Cuca).

Ciego de Ávila and Camagüey

This province, whose capital of the same name has less than 100,000 inhabitants, is one of the flattest regions of Cuba, saved from oblivion by fishing and water sports in its keys to the north and south.

Like Ciego de Ávila, Camagüey is all flatland, and once more, the sea to the north and south of the province is of major interest. The City of Camagüey, with more than 300,000 inhabitants, features both a spirited *ambiente* and a colonial setting, and is yet to be besieged by tourists.

Las Tunas

Even fewer tourists stay in the Province of Las Tunas, whose capital city has a population of above 100,000. But don't be fooled. The people are as friendly as can be and the undeveloped beaches are reserved for romantics or lovers of solitude.

Holguín and Granma

The Provinces of Holguín to the north (birthplace of Fidel Castro) and Granma to the south, occupy the same north-south slice of the island, and mark the beginning of Cuba's "fin." These two provinces also share a rugged mountainous area that includes the Sierra Maestra and other lesser ranges. The Sierra Maestra's hideaways were a perfect refuge for Castro's guerrilla army.

Both provinces are embellished with modern resorts and superb scenery. The city of Holguín has a quarter of a million people, while Granma's capital, Bayamo, is more typical in size of Cuba's provincial capitals, with less than 150,000. Bayamo is a good place to get away from the tourist subculture, while taking in the history of the country's first independence insurgent, Carlos Manuel de Céspedes, in Parque Céspedes.

The most adventurous feature of the Province of Granma, shared with the panhandle of the Province of Santiago, is the Gran Parque Nacional Sierra Maestra, whose entrance is at Alto de Naranjo. Hikers will enjoy wooded trails with spectacular views, historic sites from the Cuban Revolution, and highland rain forest scenery. It takes three days of hiking from Alto de Naranjo to the coast at Las Cuevas in the Province of Santiago, and those who plan to do the whole trip should hire a guide.

Father and son in neighborhood bar, Santiago de Cuba.

Santiago

The Province of Santiago shares the end of Cuba's fin with Guantánamo. If you fancy what is old, African, musical, and mountainous, Santiago is the perfect place. With nearly a half million inhabitants, Santiago de Cuba is the country's second city. Fewer dollars make it to Santiago inhabitants, so visitors who look like foreigners will have to deal with the human contradictions of the two-tiered economy, in the form of creative street hustlers.

Most of Cuba's revolutions began in Santiago, the site of the Moncada Barracks attacked by Fidel Castro's guerrillas. Pico Turquino and Gran Piedra are challenging hikes taking you up to cooler climates.

Guantánamo

The mountainous province of Guantánamo is the setting for the famous song *La Guantanamera* as well as the United States naval base (the only place on the island where you can buy a Big Mac). There is no access from the Cuban mainland to Guantánamo Naval Base.

The dry south coast, laden with cactus, looks out of place in Cuba, and contrasts with the lush north coast of the same province and its hauntingly beautiful colonial town of Baracoa. The south coast city of Guantánamo has more than 200,000 inhabitants, but the scenery of the north coast countryside is more attractive to most visitors.

Isla de la Juventud

Although Isla de la Juventud (Isle of Youth) is too sparsely populated to be labeled a province, it is the second largest island of the Cuban archipelago, an unspoiled spot on the earth for scuba diving or just plain meditation, with Indian cave paintings at Punta del Este, and Galápagos-type wildlife of turtles, lizards, and sea birds on the surrounding coral keys. Both José Martí and Fidel Castro were imprisoned here.

These brush-stroke descriptions of Cuba's provinces are intended as a convenient overview, so that readers may choose which settings (according to their persuasions) merit further investigation. (If you like mountains, for example, you will prefer Santiago over Camagüey.) Encyclopedic lists of churches, museums, and resorts rarely help to capture the essence of a place. Cuba's network of tourist services, from the specialty agency in your home country to on-the-spot tourism offices, provides all the needed pamphlets; regional guide booklets are available in all hotels and airports.

Chapter Three

PEOPLE

THE OLD NEIGHBORHOOD

Cuba is a country of neighborhoods. Political forums and elections thrive at the neighborhood level. The health care system is based on the neighborhood family doctor who must live on the street where he works, often in the same building of the local clinic. Even a big metropolis like Havana is comprised of many smaller "towns," with all the advantages of belonging to a social network and all the disadvantages of everyone knowing what you're doing.

Forget Privacy

There's a saying in Spanish: *Pueblo chico infierno grande* (small town, big hell). If you come from a culture that values solitude and privacy, you'll have to adjust to Cuba's incessant social interaction.

"It can get pretty intense," says Serge, a former Spanish student of mine and accomplished classical and jazz musician, who now specializes in Cuban music. "Morning and night you're always talking to people. My Spanish is good but sometimes I don't understand everything that's being said. What happens is that you give the impression you've understood more than you have, and this adds to the intensity."

Serge is a very communicative person, socially active, and exuberant in exchanging ideas. When he was in my Spanish class and had just become interested in Cuba, I rated him most-likely to adapt to Cuban culture. I bumped into him by chance a decade later when I went to a restaurant in Los Angeles to hear a group called Máquina Loca play Afro-Cuban music. To my surprise, there was Serge at the piano. He'd already been to Cuba three times, with more trips planned.

"I suppose you had no trouble adjusting," I said.

"I'm used to living alone," he replied. "Sometimes it can get too intense, with clinging relationships, and no time to collect your thoughts. But at the same time, that's my attraction to Cuba, where there's a sense of people helping people."

Hugo, an acquaintance of mine, recently left Cuba, disenchanted with economic hardships and in disagreement with how the government was dealing with the crisis. But he has experienced culture in the United States, and glowingly contrasts the Cuban spirit of neighborhood with his depersonalized suburban setting in California.

"On days off, we left our doors open. Neighbors would stroll in to chat. If someone in the neighborhood was in need, we would all make sure that he was taken care of."

In order to integrate within Cuban life, visitors who may not be accustomed to a such a people-oriented existence should give up illusions of privacy and make it a point to hang out in one neighborhood and become part of the society.

The Prado

My choice of turf was a few blocks from the *Punta* (the Point) on the Malecón, just outside of what used to be the rampart that surrounded Old Havana. The Prado, where I resided, was the first avenue to be built when Havana spilled outside of the rampart. Today it is one of the city's many outdoor living rooms. Its wide promenade resembles La Rambla in Barcelona. On either side of the promenade are two lanes for automobiles. Outside the vehicle lanes are sidewalks covered by pillared arcades.

Both the outer sidewalks and the inner *paseo* have built-in stone benches or steps to encourage social interaction. Live oaks provide plenty of shade from the tropical sun, and big light globes hang from wrought iron lamp posts. The Prado is a tangible metaphor for a section of the traditional Cuban dance, the *danzón*, called the *paseo,* in which the dancing stops and the participants stroll around and get to know each other.

Today, on a typical stroll along El Prado, it is common for people on the benches to make eye contact with a stroller and invite him or

Typical Old Havana architecture.

71

her to chat. As can be imagined, someone who looks like a foreigner is especially sought after.

My neighborhood had a number of features typical of many Cuban neighborhoods. American urbanologist Ray Oldenburg has written about the social value of family-run enterprises, as opposed to absentee ownership. In Cuba, the law requires private enterprises with no connection to the state to be family run. No employees.

Along El Prado and in the funky colonial streets of Old Havana to the west and Central Havana to the east, any time you engage in commerce, you will be doing so with the proprietor or family members with a social investment in their business. Commerce becomes personal engagement.

An Informal Economy

On the surface, it appears as if not much commerce exists, prompting observers from neon cultures to note a drabness in the scene. The absence of electric signs and colorful billboards takes much of the exterior glitz out of business, but every imaginable type of thriving commerce exists at a human scale.

In a used book store, just around the corner from my residence, you deal with the owner when asking about a book. At an outdoor beauty parlor (a table and chair on the sidewalk), you receive your manicure from a beautician who takes a direct interest in your satisfaction because she is the owner. If one feels too ill to go to a medical clinic, the doctor, who knows everybody personally within the urban quadrant he's responsible for, will pay you a visit. In fact, if he hasn't seen you in a long time, he'll probably find the time to knock on your door just to see if you're doing okay.

There are restaurants galore, but few have signs. They are labeled *paladares* (places of taste) to differentiate them from traditional restaurants. By word of mouth, you find out which apartment buildings have a *paladar*, and you will be attended to by the owner and the cook, who are probably the same person. A full-course dinner can run anywhere from US $2 to US $10. An alternative is a home-cooked meal in the underground economy beginning for roughly the equivalent of a dollar in Cuban pesos to several times as much.

One makes haphazard distinctions between the formal and the informal economy since formal businesses "look" informal in a home-spun way. The characters involved in the thriving informal economy constitute a subculture that is enthralling for anyone who places a value on creative hustling. The names have been changed to protect the characters but the essence of this informal economy follows. Carlitos, for example, has appropriated one street corner where he is available to meet your every need. In particular, he excels at securing discount taxis. A ride with an "independent" taxi will cost about 30 percent less than the official government taxi service. If Carlitos gets to know you, he'll want to chat with you about potential business ideas.

Then there is Celia, a university literature teacher who finds an occasional "date" as a *jinetera* to balance her household budget and add a few calories to her slim figure.

More than a few young men, many of them with "friends" in tobacco or rum factories, are out selling cigars and bottles of rum. It's not all business with these disgruntled citizens; if the foreigner they've approached is not interested in any of their products, they still want to sit down and chat, mainly asking questions about his or her country and explaining how tough it is to make ends meet.

Julio and Manuel are young men who get commissions from local restaurants by finding clients, and then play basketball at the local gym every night.

Amelia is one of the many women who cook creole dishes in their homes for "whatever you'd like to pay." Amelia's dinners are quite special, with a choice of chicken or pork (cooked in bitter orange and garlic), yucca (a tuber cooked with garlic), *congris* (rice with beans), and a varied salad featuring cucumber and delicious Cuban avocados. She'll also rent you her bedroom and move down a rickety spiral staircase to sleep on her living room couch.

You'll pass by street level windows, from which pizza, fruit punch, ice cream or coffee are sold. Most of these places are part of the above-ground economy and pay taxes. But the money changer who takes a one-peso commission per dollar exchanged does not work with official approval. Once you get to know him, if exact change cannot be made, he'll spot you the difference and trust that you'll come by later with the balance.

Then there are the roving musicians who play for tips. They play and sing either romantic *boleros* or *guajira* country music. These trios are usually composed of a guitar, a bongo player, and a lead singer, also a guitarist, with all three joining in to harmonize in the chorus. The tapes they sell, for about five dollars, are not recorded under ideal studio conditions.

Faced with private competition, government-run commerce is improving. A few interesting neighborhood lunch spots and bars have opened up, catering to the Cuban peso crowd. A Mayabe Beer runs for about 60 percent (in Cuban pesos) of what it costs in the nearby dollar-operated hotels.

You'll also be accosted by a man with a briefcase full of documentation on Cuban government abuses. He's an itinerant Jehovah's Witness, but everyone refers to him as *El Loco*.

Other features adding spice to the old neighborhood are the bicycle-taxi carriages, the monstrous two-humped camel buses pulled by truck cabins, the vintage automobiles, including an occasional Edsel, the ubiquitous bicycles, which mellow the sound setting compared to the auto-congested neighborhoods in other Latin American capitals, and the Malecón happening, with hustlers, kids diving off the sea wall into the slurping ocean, and the fishermen, some of whom come up with prized catches that provide a few days of dinner.

Across the strait from the Malecón is El Morro, the fortress that protected Havana against pirates during the colonial period, as seen in this illustration of a 1762 map. On the illustrated map, the center of my neighborhood runs along the rampart to La Punta (on the map

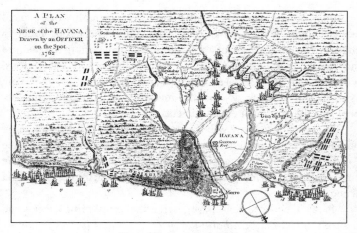

Map of Havana from 1762.

labeled "Puntal"). As Havana began to expand, the Prado was built roughly parallel to the rampart.

Today, one may transport a bicycle through a tunnel under the bay via the *ciclobus*, a bus with a specially-equipped bicycle ramp. Once on the other side, ride up to El Morro, or pedal along the coast against the pungent sea breeze all the way to Playas del Este, the favorite beach recreational spot for Havana's throngs.

It was on the Malecón where I met Felipe. On his days off, Felipe, an X-ray technician, will be looking for tourists to guide around the city with his impeccable English. Like the youthful cigar vendors, Felipe will have lots of bad things to say about the Maximum Leader, but at the same time, he and the other gripers will have nothing but praise for Che Guevara and the original intentions of the Cuban revolution. After you've heard the conversation once, you might as well make carbon copies:

"It's time for Fidel to step down," said Felipe, within earshot of a policeman. "It's a shame that we lost El Che. Cuba would have been different today if El Che had stayed with us."

Whatever the inevitable changes in Cuba, the reality of a typical late-twentieth century urban Cuban neighborhood is not about to change. The strong sense of community, a Cuban custom long before the revolution but nurtured by post-1959 neighborhood institutions, will remain. The informal economy, a necessity under any economic system, will continue to operate, mutating to fit within whatever becomes the dominant economic current.

The formal economy will continue to function as well, at a more human level than in more corporate nations. Even detractors of the Cuban system who come from countries dominated by corporate enterprise reserve a few good words for this aspect of the neighborhood scene.

"Part of Cuba's current charm," writes a sharply-critical Raymond Schroth in *National Catholic Reporter*, "is that it lacks the junk— McDonald's architecture and fast-food plastic and Styrofoam in the gutters, waste, the consumption ethic, the relentless assault of advertising."

The Malecón: one of Havana's greatest hangouts.

Substituting for corporate advertising is what Cuban exile Tony Mendoza refers to as *la búsqueda* (the search), which is how people survive in the informal economy by seeking clients for cigars, rum, impromptu tours, informal home-made lunches, outdoor beauty salons, and sex.

"Everyone has to *resolver* (to solve, or make ends meet)," writes Mendoza, who is bitterly critical of the Cuba of 1997, after he visited for the first time after 37 years of exile.

In the *Chronicle of Higher Education* Mendoza urges Cuba to open itself up to modern, capitalistic growth. "People rode bicycles everywhere, reminding me of old newsreels of Asian countries. My cabdriver drove me past 1940s- and 1950s-models of cars; I felt as if I were in a time warp."

My old Cuban neighborhood is indeed a time warp. Old Havana, protected by the revolution's laws against property speculation, remained intact long enough to be labeled by the United Nations as a patrimony of humanity.

But if Cubans suddenly struck gold and were able to exchange their bicycles for automobiles, we would all choke to death in the narrow streets of Old Havana. And if fast food outlets were to replace family-owned *paladares*, where would we again find home-made cooking with personal service? If the automobile culture were to take over Cuba as it has in my own country, would people still hang out in their old neighborhoods? Or would Havana metamorphose into a typical Latin American capital, pockmarked with glass box skyscrapers and plagued by crime, corruption, and pollution?

Sense of Community

Mendoza's time warp culture shock is ironic; in his own adopted country, the United States, many citizens are in the process of reconsidering social policy and turning back the clock to the days when personal contact and sense of community were more prevalent, and are opposing knee-jerk municipal decisions to knock down buildings of character and replace them with windowless boxes and parking structures.

Mendoza took 80 rolls of black and white photographs. In Cuban neighborhoods like mine, even color photos of groups of people come out in black and white. Had he toted his camera in urban neighborhoods in Midwest cities like Chicago, St. Louis, and Detroit, some of his photos of the people would have come out in all black and the others in all white. The buildings and automobiles in Cuba may look like a time warp but the integration between black and white is a contemporary phenomenon that Mendoza chose to ignore.

Without the personal and domestic comforts Mendoza was accustomed to in Cuba before he left at the age of 18 and now in the United States as well, what do Cuban people do? They hang out on the Prado or the street corner or the Malecón with each other. They attend neighborhood forums and street festivals. Corner bars and parks become public gathering places. This is the old-fashioned sense of community that seduces people from more modernized cultural settings to visit a place like Cuba.

Serge, my musician friend from Los Angeles, who, like Mendoza and Schroth, is no fan of Fidel Castro, prefers to bypass political agendas and evaluate Cuba from a cultural standpoint. Given the richness and variety of Cuban music, I asked Serge "what was your greatest musical experience in Cuba?"

"My whole experience in Cuba was a musical experience. Just hanging out. Not necessarily attending performances. The whole vibe, the hang, it's a soulful place."

"One of my culture contrasts was returning to Miami, to the Cuban neighborhood there," Serge added. "You just don't feel the soul, that *ambiente*. It's almost shocking!"

LITERARY BORDER CROSSINGS

The crossing of cultural borders is a recurring theme in a rich array of literary works by remarkable personalities who represent different aspects of the Cuban experience. Nicolás Guillén's poetry confronts the dilemma of the Cuban poet's dual heritage of Africa and Spain, and intersects culturally with African-American poet Langston Hughes, an admirer and translator of Guillén.

Alejo Carpentier's exile to Europe, return to Cuba, and subsequent diplomatic posts abroad allow him to view Latin American cultures from both beyond and within, and at least one of his novels, *The Lost Steps*, makes culture shock a primary theme.

Assata Shakur is not Cuban by birth, but has lived in Cuba for more than two decades as an exile from the United States. *Assata: An Autobiography* culminates with her adjustment to the Cuban way of life following her daring escape from prison in the United States.

The criterion for choosing to profile these three authors in place of so many other Cuban and foreigner literary personalities with ties to Cuba is that they feature the theme of crossing cultural boundaries. Had space allowed, other luminaries could have received equal billing.

But literary celebrities like Hemingway have been portrayed again and again in books on Cuba and are now the object of tourist schlock. Although Hemingway once shook hands with Fidel Castro and had denounced Batista, he had no involvement in the changes occurring in Cuba at the time he left. Perhaps it was a terminal illness that left this great reporter oblivious to the type of dramatic story he thrived on. He had left a very public existence in Havana in order to commit the most private of all acts. A year after his departure from Cuba, in the empty expanses of Idaho, he put a loaded rifle to his head and pressed the trigger.

Any visitor to Cuba will bump into relics of Hemingway's Havana period. But tourists come and go without engaging in the insights of the three literary figures portrayed in the following pages.

Double Deception: Nicolás Guillén and Langston Hughes

Can two people be born into two different cultures and yet grow up like doubles, carving out an identical path in life? Langston Hughes was born in the United States in 1902. Nicolás Guillén was born the same year in Cuba. Both Hughes and Guillén were of African heritage in segregated societies. Both were able to break through racial barriers and attend Ivy League universities. But both would drop out of college to pursue careers as writers and poets. Within the poetic output of both of these artists was a commitment to social justice. But as these kindred spirits reached the age of 28, they had never met.

When cruise lines Cunard, Panamá Pacific, and United Fruit all refused to sell Hughes a ticket to Cuba in 1930, one of the ticket sellers told the U.S. poet that there was a ban against blacks traveling to Cuba. Hughes checked with the Cuban embassy, where he was told that no such ban existed.

Hughes wanted to travel to Cuba with his "rusty but serviceable Spanish" to obtain documentation on Cuban music for an Afro-American opera project. A trip to Cuba would also set the stage for an encounter with Nicolás Guillén. Thanks to the intervention of a white friend of Hughes, the poet was able to purchase an expensive stateroom ticket on Cunard's ship, *Caronia*. Hughes was not sure if he could mix with the passengers, until, according to biographer Arnold Rampersad, "he found relief that they [the passengers] were mostly Jewish."

In Havana, Langston Hughes was "amused to see clothes hanging out to dry on top of buildings" (and today, you'll see the same sights over the balconies in Old Havana). More shocking than the clothing draped out to dry was the criticism of Hughes's host, José Antonio Fernández de Castro, editor of *El Diario de la Marina*. Fernández spoke to Hughes about Yankee imperialism, the self-proclaimed U.S. right to intervene militarily in Cuba, and absentee ownership of much of Cuban agriculture and industry by North Americans. Fernández was the first person to translate Hughes's poetry into Spanish. He walked Hughes down the Prado boulevard, where "everyone wanted to be introduced to the greatest Negro poet in the United States and the world."

Hughes went to hear the Cuban *son* at the all-black Club Atenas, where he became a hit with the *sonero* musicians. Like the blues, the *son* had emerged from traditional African culture. Hughes had done much to publicize Afro-Cuban music abroad and hoped that a leading Cuban composer, Amadeo Roldán, would be his partner in the Afro-American opera project. But the light-skinned Roldán resented being referred to as black or Negro. Hughes reacted with disgust and immediately became skeptical about Cuban claims of racial harmony.

Hughes still looked forward to meeting Nicolás Guillén, the mulatto poet who had written with pride of his African heritage. Without having known each other, Hughes and Guillén had uncanny poetic affinities.

Following their first meeting, Langston Hughes felt sufficient rapport with his counterpart to share specific ideas about Guillén's poetry. At their second get-together, he recommended that Guillén make the rhythms of the Afro-Cuban *son,* the authentic music of the black masses, central to his poetry, as Hughes had done with blues and jazz. Guillén's next book, *Motivos de Son*, did just that. From then on, Hughes and Guillén became friends, and their poetry seemed to emanate from a united soul.

Since Hughes was a supporter of the civil rights movement in the United States, Nicolás Guillén expected his friend to raise a voice of support against the *"vandálicos hechos"* of the Bay of Pigs invasion in 1961. Segregation in Cuba had ended with the revolution, and for the first time in his life, Guillén, as a man of African heritage, felt free, as expressed in his now classic poem *Tengo* (I Have). As the president of the Cuban Association of Writers and Artists, Guillén implored Hughes for vocal support against another potential U.S. invasion.

Langston Hughes had been in a similar situation when he'd asked for support from composer Amadeo Roldán, only to be met by Roldán's reticence to take a stand in favor of his African heritage. Now it was Hughes, one of the greatest U.S. poets of the twentieth century, who was asked to take a stand. Fearlessly, Hughes had written against racial oppression, at a time when it was not popular to do so.

Hughes rejected Guillén's request, however. One of his biographers suggests that he did so out of fear of personal reprisal. Hughes was aware that two U.S. poets had lost their jobs after traveling to Castro's Cuba.

But Langston Hughes was not one to walk away from an issue. His poetry itself was threatening to the U.S. establishment. For example, Educator Jonathan Kozol was fired from his teaching job after having read a Langston Hughes poem to his black students in the Boston school system. The poem was considered inflammatory and revolutionary by the Boston school board.

In fairness to Langston Hughes, the anti-Cuba atmosphere in the United States came on the heels of McCarthyist blacklisting, and Hughes was well aware that African-Americans had always been most vulnerable to political reprisals. But it is doubtful that individual concerns were the motive for the courageous Hughes to leave his friend Nicolás Guillén in the wake. The civil rights movement in the United States, Hughes's great struggle, was being falsely criticized by white supremacists as "communist influenced." Any potential Langston Hughes declaration against U.S. intervention in Cuba would have been used as propaganda to undermine the civil rights movement.

Nicolás Guillén, who died in 1989, is today considered Cuba's national poet, and anyone considering traveling to Cuba would do well to read and enjoy his poetry.

Alejo Carpentier: The Lost Steps

Alejo Carpentier (1904–1980) was one of Cuba's great twentieth century novelists. After imprisonment by the Machado regime, Carpentier spent many years in exile, returning to Cuba after the revolution. He was nominated for a Nobel Prize several times and his baroque prose has a cult of devotees. Carpentier was also a journalist, radio station director, musicologist, composer, history teacher, and the head of a national publishing company.

It is a custom in Latin America to hand out choice diplomatic posts to great writers as a scholarship that enables them to continue producing their art. Carpentier was offered the post of ambassador in Paris but preferred the lesser position of cultural attaché.

The Cuban novel recommended to me the most by Cuban lovers of literature is Carpentier's *The Lost Steps (Los Pasos Perdidos)*, written in 1956. A standard review of this truly magnificent novel would emphasize the plot line: a music composer living in an unnamed European country is given funds by a museum curator to travel to the remote jungles of an unnamed Latin American country in order to track down the most basic and original instruments: the source of music itself.

The unnamed protagonist's actress wife is too busy with her career to maintain an ongoing relationship. Mouche, an astrologist girl friend, very much like one of today's New Agers, tags along with him for the adventure. Among the many obstacles along the way is a prototypical Latin American coup d'état that traps the two lovers in their hotel.

The change of culture (the protagonist is returning to the land where he was raised) is cause for discord between the lovers. On the way from the city to the jungle, the protagonist meets an earthy local woman who is much less intellectual than his European companion but whose homespun philosophy is much more authentic.

Carpentier was a Renaissance man, and everything from his eclectic background finds its way into the novel, which becomes as dense as the rain forest explored by the protagonist. With so much there, the novel reads like the façade of a baroque church. Its intricate detail causes the reader to stop and contemplate, while its flowing story moves on relentlessly like the Orinoco River that inspires it.

Within the "culture shock" perspective, *The Lost Steps'* subplot is pivotal for anyone with a western cultural heritage who wishes to travel into the depths of Latin America, Cuba included.

Carpentier's life had one foot in Europe and the other in Cuba, and the cultural contrasts he perceives between the two continents may anticipate experiences of some travelers today. Others will take issue with Carpentier's point of view, as it is reflected by his protagonist.

The protagonist's European wife is so career-oriented that she has little time for her husband. He writes about the "hardness ... of that city of perennial anonymity within the multitude, of that eternal haste, where eyes only met by chance, and a smile, when coming from a stranger, always concealed a pragmatic motive."

The protagonist becomes upset at being stereotyped by his lady friend Mouche, who "would attribute the *animalness* of my reactions to my early upbringing, which took place in a Latin American setting."

Mouche's difficulty in adjusting to Latin American culture results from her view of the people's customs as exotic rather than normal. "An aura of exoticism thickened around her, establishing distances between her figure and the figures of others." She suffered from a typical case of culture shock.

As the protagonist becomes more and more settled within the culture of his upbringing, his lover seems ever more foreign to him. However, the protagonist's new lady friend, Rosario, is also culturally removed from him. "When I looked at her as a woman, I felt clumsy, inhibited, conscious of my own exoticism ... there were the thousands books I'd read that she was unaware of; there were her beliefs, customs, superstitions, notions that I was unaware of and that, even so, represented reasons for living as valid as my own."

The Lost Steps, then, is also the story of a dramatic cultural tug-of-war, with the protagonist caught between two very distinct world views.

The apparent dichotomy between contemporary and traditional cultures is made out to be a mere cliché by Carpentier. Mouche may seem liberated, in the modern western sense, but she is imprisoned by the custom of analyzing what should be left to nature. Rosario is a traditional woman who wants to serve; when speaking to the narrator she calls herself *your woman*. But when it comes to their intimate relationship, she does not let analytical inhibitions get in the way and prefers to surrender to "the joy of the body." Yet, she is fiercely independent, and does not see her reason for living as bound to her lover.

"According to her [Rosario], marriage, the legal binding, steals a woman's recourse for defending herself against men," a statement that coincidentally reflects the view of many of today's Cuban women.

Another cultural contradiction faced by the narrator concerns his own tendency to live for the future, a posture that clashes with a way of life in a remote village in which present tense survival is everything.

The narrator's actress wife and his benefactor, the curator, are both perplexed when he does not return to Europe. Believing him to be lost in the jungle, they dispatch a plane on a rescue mission. The narrator would prefer to remain in the remote village situated at the beginning of time and music, writing an elaborate musical composition that will probably never be performed.

But his cultural transformation is incomplete, bound as he is to his past, and when the plane lands and the pilot finds him, the narrator must make a decision of enormous consequences, based on his conflicting feelings about the two radically different cultures that now struggle for control of his spirit.

The Lost Steps is one of the great novels of the twentieth century, whose most exciting theme, often overlooked by the critics, is the dramatic clash between two ways of life within one human being. Anyone who travels from one culture to another will greatly benefit from a reading of this Cuban masterpiece.

An American Refugee in Havana: Assata Shakur

Most of us will not experience the same culture shock in Cuba as Assata Shakur. But few people arrive in Havana after such an intense and turbulent past.

"If i [sic] sit and add up all the 'colored' toilets and drinking fountains in my life and all of the back-of-the-buses or the Jim Crow railroad cars or the places I couldn't go, it adds up to one great ball of anger," wrote Assata Shakur in her *Assata: An Autobiography*.

Only the last chapter of Shakur's gripping narration occurs in Havana, but it is a revealing chapter, where her perceptions of Cuba are better understood in the context of what happened before. Shakur's book is an intellectual-political history of the events that lead up to her imprisonment on charges of murdering a New Jersey state trooper, and her daring escape from the maximum security wing of the Clinton Correctional Facility for Women in New Jersey in 1979.

After an early childhood in the segregated south that included death threats from white vigilantes who harassed her grandparents' beachfront business, Assata's mother moved her north to New York, where she would confront the typical self-hatred of a black youth who wanted to look more like the white celebrities she'd see on typical fifties sitcoms like *Ozzie and Harriet.*

Her personal transformation, in the context of the black political movement of the sixties and early seventies, included a discarding of the humiliating hair alterations on the outside and a fierce pride in her African heritage within.

Feisty Assata admits that her stubbornness was often to blame for conflicts with her school teacher mother, and her beloved aunt, who also became her lawyer. But most of her rage is directed against racism.

Assata participated with a myriad of anti-racist and Black nationalist groups. She ended up with the Black Panthers, volunteering in their breakfast program for school children, as well as other educational and health care activities in black neighborhoods. Her interest in school children was stimulated by her own childhood experiences when white teachers treated her paternalistically, expecting less from her because she was black, and resenting it when she would question the text-book clichés about heroes like George Washington and Abraham Lincoln.

Her joining the Black Panthers was ill-timed, occurring precisely at the time when the FBI, through its now infamous COINTELPRO program, was "attempting to destroy the Black Panther Party in particular and the Black Liberation Movement in general."

Assata gained fame as a revolutionary, and it seemed that every time a black woman was involved in a bank robbery, Assata would be wanted. Assata, the former JoAnne Chesimard, was eventually acquitted of a fantastic array of bank robbery, kidnapping, and drug charges. In one case, her accuser admitted in court that he was a police informant and the charges were dropped. In other instances, the case against her was dismissed as frivolous.

But one charge stuck. On a fateful night on the New Jersey Turnpike in 1973, Assata was riding with two male companions and their car was stopped by New Jersey troopers. Shooting erupted. In the shoot-out, her friend Zayd and a state trooper died. She was convicted of being an accomplice to murder by an all-white jury. The evidence was questionable, however.

In 1979, seven international jurists visited United States prisons, and they listed Assata Shakur as a "political prisoner ... a class of victims of FBI misconduct through the COINTELPRO strategy and other forms of illegal government conduct who as political activists have been selectively targeted for provocation, false arrests, entrapment, fabrication of evidence, and spurious criminal prosecutions." The report added: "One of the worst cases is that of ASSATA SHAKUR ..."

Her narration reads like a combination of *The Shawshank Redemption* and Malcolm X's autobiography, with trial scenes as dramatic as the best scenes in John Grisham novels, and with powerful yet lyrical poems at the end of each chapter.

After Assata Shakur's tribulations, her immediate appreciation of Havana was entirely expected. But she arrived in Cuba predisposed to be sharply critical of community and race relations, her area of passionate expertise.

"The first thing that hit me were the open doors. Everywhere you go doors are open wide. You see people inside their homes talking, working, or watching television. I was amazed to find that you could actually walk down the streets at night alone." Having done volunteer work in the areas of health and education, she could be expected to embrace Cuba's free health care and equal educational opportunities.

But it is in the area of race relations where Shakur's opinions are most in demand. "Nowhere did I find a segregated neighborhood, but several people told me that where I was living had been all white before the Revolution. Just from casual observation it was obvious that race relations in Cuba were different from what they were in the u.s. Blacks and whites could be seen together everywhere—in cars, walking down streets. Kids of all races played together. It was definitely different."

But Shakur remained "skeptical and suspicious" when people told her that there was no racism in Cuba. She found it peculiar that people of African origin could declare "I am Cuban" with no need for icons from their African origins to boost their self-esteem.

She was confused by Cuba's racial categories, especially by the term mulatto. "I'm not a mulatto, but a Black woman, and I'm proud to be Black," she would explain to Cubans. "All of my associations with the word 'mulatto' were negative," she wrote. "It represented slavery, slave owners raping Black women ... In some Caribbean countries, it represented the middle level of a hierarchical, three caste system—the caste that acted as a buffer class between the white rulers and the Black masses ... i felt that the mulatto thing hindered Cubans from dealing with some of the negative ideas left over from slavery."

She later understood that "in some ways, Cubans and I approached the problem from different angles ... I respected the Cuban government, not only for adopting nonracist principles, but for struggling to put these principles in practice." When Cubans are so moved to identify themselves by color, a very infrequent occurrence, they do so nonchalantly, the way one describes a car as red or a slice of squash is yellow. (Latin Americans are more straight forward about physical appearance in general, and nicknames that would be considered racist or of a mocking nature in many English-speaking countries simply represent a recognition of physical reality in much of Latin America. A woman, for example, can call her husband *gordito* in a loving way. But in an English-speaking country, no one calls a companion "fatty," the English meaning of *gordito*.)

Assata Shakur did find one man who had objected to his white daughter marrying a black man. But the father of the bride was eventually won over. Shakur did not expect that all racism could be overcome from one decade to the next.

Assata Shakur is happy with her adjustment to Cuba, although "It was hard in the beginning, because I had to adjust to another culture and learn another language. I had to adjust to living in a Third World country, which means that things people in the U.S. take for granted— like hot running water whenever you turn on the tap—are not always available here."

References to Assata Shakur's pre-Havana life were necessary in order that we empathize with her adjustment to Cuba. We've already met several visitors to Cuba who found the life so intense that they needed to get away for a break. But Shakur's life was so intense in the United States that "Another thing I've been able to do in Cuba," she says, "is to rest."

Shakur appreciates Cuba's sense of community (the Panther's were a community-oriented organization) and the absence of racial conflict. This has allowed her to do things she'd never had time for in her other existence, such as writing fiction and painting.

"I'm crafting a vision of my life that involves creativity. And Cuban society allows me to do this."

In particular, Shakur feels liberated by being able to express her feelings of vulnerability and sensitivity. In Cuba, there is no need for wearing a protective psychological mask. "I can cry and be human and lean on people who take care of me. That can be very liberating."

While she has been gone, the African-American struggle has changed, but Assata's vocabulary and political positions remain unabashedly rooted in the late sixties and early seventies. During her political exile, several of her Panther colleagues in U.S. jails have been granted new trials or are the objects of intense campaigns for their release. In the meantime, Assata Shakur has adjusted just fine to Cuban culture. In her early fifties, she keeps fit by jogging. If plans for a Cuban film about her life are fulfilled, we may get to see more of Assata Shakur in Cuba.

Chapter Four

ENCOUNTERS

STRANGERS IN PARADISE

I arrived late one afternoon in Los Angeles with two children and no place to stay. I'd been hired by a university to teach Latin American literature and had been told that a good place to live was Culver City.

I parked my Ford on a street in Culver City near a public phone and began checking out apartment-for-rent ads from the local throw-away newspaper. The sun was setting and time was running out before I'd have to hole up in a hotel, a difficult proposition with two young kids who needed a place with a kitchen and home-cooked food.

A lady in the neighborhood, chubby and middle-aged, with a rasping voice and a bright smile, a granddaughter tugging at her apron, noticed we were ambling around. She asked where we were from, in a Spanish accent. I responded in Spanish, and after a few minutes of animated small talk, in which my apartment search was the primary theme, she volunteered a solution.

"Why don't you stay with us for the night, so you'll be able to look for apartments without so much pressure?"

Essentially, she had offered a total stranger a room in her house, just like that. Celia was from Cuba. I wondered if all Cuban people were so trusting of strangers.

She told me how she hated Fidel and how she was so happy to have fled from Cuba. But when the issue of schools for my children came up, she mentioned the disturbing social problems in her daughter's nearby high school. "What we need here is a Fidel!" she said.

A few years later, in Bolivia, my wife and I went to eat in a Cuban restaurant, owned by a recent arrival from Cuba. I was preparing for my first trip to Havana and was immersing myself in Cuban culture. The restaurant was closed due to an illness in the family. Arnulfo, the owner, was on the premises, and apologized for not being able to serve us.

"But let me invite the two of you to a *mojito*" (a typical Cuban drink). Although we had not known Arnulfo before, he told us about his sister's health problems and how an incorrect diagnosis in Washington had prompted her to come to Bolivia. Soon, Arnulfo was sharing his personal devastation over his sister's brain tumor, the terrible side effects of the medication prescribed in Washington, and the latest diagnosis in Bolivia by a Cuban doctor that there was no such tumor and that the medication itself was the cause of her fainting spells.

These were things that close friends or family members talk about. Arnulfo was telling all to strangers.

CONVERSATIONS

Upon my arrival in Cuba, I soon realized that my encounters with Celia and Arnulfo were typical of the Cuban custom of immediate and profound communication with strangers. In school in the United States, my children had been taught about Stranger Danger, but it seems as if Cubans are brought up to consider strangers as friends until the evidence indicates the contrary.

One American tourist driving through the Escambray mountains was beset by car trouble and was stranded at the side of the road. Thanks to the mishap, he explained, "I ended up with a personal guide for the rest of my vacation and was guest of honor at a local wedding."

In a country that strives to eliminate the fundamental uncertainties in life, the chance factor is embraced in the realm of human relationships.

Seika, a young Japanese woman studying Spanish and art in Cuba, was "shocked" by "how people immediately talk with you. If one has something to say he'll immediately join the conversation. There is no hesitation. This thing impressed me much in my early days in Cuba. Why do people talk to others so easily? They often say *compañero* to each other. I think this sense of companionship gives them more friendships among strangers.

"They ask anything they want to know and give their own suggestions whether you like it or not. It goes like this: 'You've had your hair cut short, but I prefer it longer. You must not have it cut next time.'

"I would like to say 'That's none of your business,' but anyhow, they mean no harm. Although their insensitiveness sometimes makes me irritated, I've given up because they care about others in any way and any means. They seldom leave me alone. It's difficult to be wholly lonely here."

Gina Margillo, a health educator from San Francisco, California, has the same impression.

"I'd never been to the Caribbean before. The openness of the people, the intense heat, there's an incredible kinetic energy.

"It's the Cubans' frankness. It is so surprising as to seem blunt. I didn't know what to expect, being from the United States. That didn't matter. They were eager to talk with me."

I had planned to spend some time meditating at the sea wall in Havana. If that is one of your objectives, you'd better find an empty beach. If there are people around, they will inevitably approach and begin a conversation.

In many parts of the United States, if you begin talking to strangers they think you're nuts. There is a suspicion about the unknown, about the "other," as if all outsiders must be considered as Stranger Danger until proven otherwise.

I quickly learned in Havana that if I was in a hurry for an appointment, I'd better read my map and know my streets, for if I stopped to ask directions, a conversation would ensue and I'd never get there on time.

I also learned to start out for a destination with plenty of time to spare. The people you meet along the way are going to be more interesting than any planned activity.

The trick, if there is one, is to differentiate between the hustlers who need dollars and want to sell you something, cigars, rum, free-lance tours, sex, and those who simply want to talk and get to know new people from different cultures. I was having difficulty making the distinction when I first met Soledad.

SOLEDAD

The sound of salsa music drew me away from my planned route and in the direction of an outdoor restaurant at a plaza in Old Havana. As I stood listening to Afro-Cuban layered rhythms, the chorus echoing the solo singer, and the jazzy bass guitar, a young, sweet voice asked in English if I was enjoying the salsa.

During the "Special Period in a time of peace," so many people on the street are out to sell you something that I shied away.

"*No tengas miedo*," the young black woman said, switching to Spanish. "It's our nature to talk to people."

I had heard the "*no tengas miedo*" before, an all-purpose Cuban term that let foreigners know it is normal for Cubans to talk to strangers.

"Sorry," I said, truly embarrassed about my Stranger Danger reaction. I had arrived for the last song of the outdoor jam session. The people who had been milling around outside the restaurant either went in or walked away.

"Have you seen the new art exposition?" she asked. I hadn't, and was interested in Cuban art. She led me in toward a gallery, while asking me predictable questions like, where was I from, and looked a little surprised when I told her I was a *gringo*.

Inside the exposition, we both passed on the offer of wine and hors d'oeuvres. It was a much simpler inauguration of an art exhibition than I was used to. Here the hors d'oeuvres were simple white bread sandwiches, and there was a choice of white wine or Cuban cola. The men wore embroidered *guayabera* shirts, untucked, and the women loose cotton dresses. Some of the paintings were totally abstract, others representational. Soledad was most impressed by the ones that mixed the abstract with the pictorial.

Back outside, on the narrow streets, beneath balconies with clothing drying on the railings, the afternoon heat and humidity awakened my thirst. I asked Soledad where I could buy some *refrescos* and she showed me a window of a building from which fresh fruit drinks were served in plastic cups. It was one of my first introductions to the Cuban peso economy and I was elated to see that something better than Coca Cola was available to fit the Cuban budget, for just one Cuban peso.

We took our drinks to a park across the street, about a block from the Malecón.

Soledad was a university student. She looked in her late teens but told me she was twenty-two. Along with a brother, she lived with her grandmother. Her mother, an ophthalmologist, had remarried, and I got the impression that within the extended family, the children had moved in with grandma a few blocks away, to give their honeymooning mother a little privacy. The mother was making up for what she'd lost. Her former husband had left for the United States in the 1980s, written a few letters, and then disappeared after having remarried.

It had taken Soledad awhile to get from the "where are you from?" to the "what are you doing in Cuba?" I told her that I was a specialist in Latin American Studies and I was writing a book.

Suddenly her ebullient ebony face lost its radiance and elongated, like a melancholic Modigliani. She spoke of American writers who had come to Cuba as friends and then had written vitriolic articles that denigrated *el proceso* in Cuba. (When Cubans talk about their social system, they don't mention Fidel. They refer to "the process" which is supposed to lead toward social equality. Black people like Soledad are more likely to defend "the process" since they have benefited the most from Cuba's social reforms.)

Soledad explained that she was afraid that what she said to me might be turned around into something that would harm her country.

This time it was my turn to say *No tengas miedo*, that I just wanted to write about reality, and that I wouldn't be in Cuba if I didn't have a profound love for Cuban culture.

She apologized for her reticence, but had I heard about the recent bombings of hotels and restaurants? It was another covert attempt by the United States, she said, to disrupt the Cuban economy.

"You'll have to just look at me, listen to what I have to say, and judge for yourself," I said. "Do I look like a terrorist?"

We remained on the park bench, exchanging ideas about everything under the Havana sun. I learned from this encounter that she was not the type of uncritical supporter of "the process" that I'd expected to meet. When I asked her why Cuba doesn't produce more food, she criticized the dependency on the Soviets and the lack of diversification in the economy.

"But now we are producing more food. I know because I volunteer for the student brigades that go to the country to harvest. It's not sugar anymore. We harvest things that you can eat. I enjoy the brigades. There's a great spirit and we have parties every night."

Soledad's concept of solidarity transcended the party line. I could tell by the pride with which she told of her mother's disobedience to authority. A Peruvian man had come to Cuba for an operation on his eyes. Somehow he'd run out of money before the operation. Soledad's mother was supposed to perform the surgery, but she was told by her supervisor that without payment, there could be no operation.

"She disobeyed her boss and operated on the patient anyway," Soledad said. "I'm proud of her for that."

A peanut vendor came by. Cuban peanuts, the ones they sell on the street in paper cones, are roasted crisp, and have a flavor unknown in countries that receive imported nuts. Soledad bought the peanuts and I ran across the street for some Cuban canned sodas.

The peanut lady, looking to be in her sixties, white, with sharp cheek bones on a thin face, said her name was Amelia, and that she cooked for people in her home. In spite of her age, Amelia walked off with the sprightliness of a youngster. I recalled how an old factory foreman for whom I'd worked judged the potential success of job applicants by how they walked. If Amelia cooked like she walked, then her *criollo* cooking was going to be exquisite.

"You won't be disappointed," she said on her second tour of the park. "You'll recognize my apartment building by the small food stand downstairs. That's my stand, but there I only sell snacks."

The conversation with Soledad had been so intense that I hadn't realized it was now dark. I didn't want her to be stranded without transportation and offered to walk her to her bus, which left from the Prado, a few blocks from my residence. She told me not to worry, that there were buses for at least another hour or two. We agreed to meet the next day to continue our conversation. "Why don't we go to Amelia's," I suggested.

Soledad's face turned long and somber again.

"Am I wrong about Amelia?" I asked. "She seems for real."

"It's not that," she explained. "I'm not sure it's right to patronize places like that. It's money that could have gone to a government restaurant that should go directly to the needs of the people."

This new polemic extended our conversation for another half hour. If Amelia had her stand on the street, then she was a tax payer, I asserted. Soledad admitted Cuban business was taxed steeply so that a new commercial class would not emerge to dominate others. In a way, I suggested, when we patronize a tax-paying business, the money goes directly to Cubans. "That sounds better than eating in a government sanctioned, foreign-owned hotel, where a chunk of the dividends would leave the country."

As we walked to her bus stop, I considered asking Soledad to help me with my research. I needed to do at least two hundred interviews. But I wanted them to be as diversified as possible. My idea was to employ university students to do interviews for me. Soledad seemed like an ideal candidate.

"I can't pay a lot," I said, explaining my project, "but I'd pay *en divisa*" (in U.S. dollars).

"I'm not sure about it," she said. "What I do might be used in a way that could disparage Cuba."

I was shocked. Many Cubans I'd met on the street were jumping at the chance to earn dollars, but Soledad balked at the opportunity, even though her family was among the 48 percent that had no access to dollars. "Soledad," I said. "The questions I need to ask are cultural. I'm not getting into politics."

"Between the lines of any and everything there is a message. We can talk about your idea tomorrow if you wish, but I'm afraid I might do harm, unintentionally."

She looked up and smiled, her dark skin merging with the unlit Havana night, her large, deep-set eyes shining under the street lamp. "Tomorrow we can talk about many things."

We shook hands and I kissed her on the cheek.

"In Bolivia, when we say good-bye, we kiss the woman on the cheek. Is that the custom in Cuba, too?"

"Yes, that's our custom."

I left her on an orderly line to her bus. It was the first stop on the bus route, so when she got on, there was a seat waiting for her.

JESÚS AND MICHEL

My friendship with Soledad was an encouraging sign. Cuba was in a rickety economical state, and most people were operating in survival mode, which meant getting a hold of dollars in any way they could, short of violence. But there was still hope if idealists like Soledad could turn down a chance for easy dollars on the basis of principle.

She had corroborated Assata Shakur's assertions about Cuba's racial harmony, based on the daily imagery of friendships between blacks, whites, and mulattos. As a black woman, Soledad had said, "I wouldn't think of leaving Cuba. I've heard about the racism in the United States and Spain."

With the idealism of Soledad in my mind, I strolled out to the Malecón one late afternoon to watch the sea and take in the social scene. I stood by the stone wall and watched the waveless sea caress the rocks at the outer base below.

Two young men approached, a new portrait in black and white, another image of racial harmony, and my spirits were once more lifted.

"Where are you from?" the white man asked.

Both Jesús (the lanky black man) and Michel (a shorter white man with blue-green eyes and curly brown hair) were thrilled to have the chance to talk with an "American."

They seemed in their early twenties.

"Are you in a hurry?" Michel asked. "Why don't you sit down so we can talk?"

After a few stanzas in English, we drifted back into Spanish as the substance of our discussion got heavier. Sooner or later, the subject of economic hardships came up. I asked their opinion about the embargo.

"The blockade is not the cause of our problems," Michel said.

"It's our government," Jesús agreed.

Cuban conversations seem to soar when they are based on polemics, so I took issue. "Both of you guys speak excellent English," I said. "You learned the language in high school. In my country it's rare for students to learn foreign languages in high school classes. You must have good schools."

"We're not complaining about our schools," said Jesús. "We're complaining because we're not allowed to buy and sell things as we please."

Jesús, the black man, was studying at the university and had learned French as well as English. Michel worked in a tobacco factory. They asked me where I usually ate. Politely, they suggested that if I wanted the same quality of dinner for a fraction of the price, they could take me to a place where they received a commission. It was a typical "arrangement" within the underground economy.

"By letting us help you, you'll be helping us."

When I found out how inexpensive the food was going to be, I realized that I could invite both of them and still get off for less than what it had cost me at my favorite *paladar*.

My conversation with Jesús and Michel was the cynical antithesis of what I'd heard from Soledad, although with the same friendly exuberance. "You know there's racism in Cuba," Michel said. Righteous indignation seemed to flow out from the green in his sparkling eyes. The fact that a white man felt such indignation about racism, I thought, was a positive sign.

"When a black and a white guy are on the street, the cops stop the black guy and leave the white man alone," Michel added.

Michel and Jesús were pouring rain on my parade of enchantment. After Soledad's lofty idealism, I wanted so hard to become a believer. And now I'd met these cynics. Warm and friendly, but cynics nonetheless.

"Well," I explained, "that's a lot like South Central L.A., except back in L.A. or Washington D.C., the whole neighborhood is black, and blacks complain that they're constantly being harassed by the cops, just because they're black." "Just looking around here," I said, "it couldn't be as bad as you say. In my country, you don't see blacks and whites hanging together all the time. What's normal here is an exception over there."

Jesús, the black man, just looked on as his friend Michel continued the diatribe, always speaking in the first person plural.

"Believe us," he smiled. "Sooner or later you'll realize that we still have racism in Cuba."

"Let's go eat," I said, wanting a reprise from the unpleasant subject. We left our perch on the stone wall by the sea and crossed the Malecón boulevard. As we reached the other side, a policeman motioned to us with his index finger.

"He's pointing at Jesús," Michel said.

Jesús walked over to the policemen, took out his wallet, and shuffled for his identification card.

"You see!" Michel whispered. "Just what we were talking about! Why didn't he stop ME? Okay, they don't like Cubans harassing foreigners. Maybe that's why they stopped Jesús. But why not me too? I may be white but don't I look just as Cuban as Jesús?"

"Maybe I can go over there and put in a good word," I suggested.

"Better not. Jesús will resolve."

As the policeman inspected Jesús's ID, I recalled the writings of a Cuban black woman, Lourdes Casal, a professor at Rutgers University. Before the revolution, she wrote, blacks were seriously underrepresented in banks, commerce, and professions.

"In Havana, upper-class social clubs excluded blacks and mulattos systematically … In Cuban small towns and provincial capitals, segregation was rigidly enforced," although it blended in with class divisions.

After the revolution, she wrote, Fidel said, "we must prioritize more and more the battle to end racial discrimination at the workplace," and he also called for ending discrimination in recreation centers by integrating public schools.

The stern-faced policeman continued to scrutinize Jesús's ID with squinting eyes.

"Privately," wrote Casals, "many white Cubans—even solid revolutionaries—employ the old racist language. The difference is

that there is a tremendous cost in expressing such prejudiced opinions publicly.

"The early redistributive measures of the Revolution improved the status of blacks in particular," added Casals. "The most far-reaching measure of equality was the elimination of private schools that had been mainly white."

"It can be unhesitatingly affirmed that racial discrimination has been solidly eradicated from Cuban society," she concluded. "This does not imply that all forms of prejudice have been banned or that the consciousness of the people has been thoroughly transformed."

Her last sentence referred directly to the policeman, who was now sending Jesús on his way. Jesús had signed some sort of paper.

He walked back to us and grinned.

"He gave me a fine," he said. "Nothing much. My documents were ragged and needed to be replaced."

"You see, Mark," insisted Michel. "Just like we said. Why didn't the cop stop *me*? Because I'm white!"

Had this been an uncanny coincidence? It almost looked like a staged performance, intended to prove the indignant accusations of Michel.

In the 1953 census prior to the revolution, 26.9 percent of Cuba's population was either black or mulatto, which seems like an undercount, since Oppenheimer refers to the 1959 unofficial total as 45 percent. But with the post-revolution white flight, Oppenheimer, citing the same unofficial source, now put Cuba's blacks and mulattos in the early 1990s at about 58 percent of the total population.

Since the onset of the Special Period, blacks comprise the majority of those Cubans who do not receive dollars from abroad. Only 5 percent of the Cuban exile community is black. The new dollar-based class divisions may therefore have an unsettling racial component.

Traditionally, Cuban uprisings have originated in the Oriente around Santiago, where Afro-Cubans are in a greater majority. One foreign diplomat in Havana told me that some whites privately fear a new black rebellion beginning in the Oriente.

Once again I had gone from one end to the other in Cuba's paradoxical spectrum. Soledad's idealism and her belief in Cuba's racial justice was the high point. But when the policeman stopped the lanky, good-natured Jesús on the street for apparently no reason, I was left with a queasy feeling in my wounded spirit.

WILLIAM

But the day had not ended. On the Prado that night, I met another young man, William, one of my neighbors. William gave a few distressing accounts about the hardships his family was enduring and then invited me to his house to meet his mother, sister, and cousins.

As in most buildings in Old Havana, the visitor goes through a dark and asymmetrical labyrinth before getting to whichever apartment is on the agenda. The door from the dark hall entered directly into a living room. William's mother, looking in her late fifties, was happy to receive a visitor from her easy chair.

She noticed that I was peering at the strange statuettes on various tables in the living room.

"Those are our saints," she said. "The African saints."

The Cuban Santería religion comes from the Yoruba culture of West Africa. I had heard that many Cubans still practice this religion, even more than Catholicism. But here in William's apartment these were white Cubans who believed in black saints.

William proudly named each of the saints.

With white people believing in a black religion, it was going to be difficult for widespread racism to make a comeback, I thought. Back on the Prado on the way home, I saw that most of the groups of people sitting around and chatting, or strolling back from the Malecón, were interracial.

The emotional roller coaster was on its way up again. But at any moment it could take another plunge.

"The jury is still out on the impact of the Cuban revolution on race relations," wrote John Burdick in "The Myth of Racial Democracy," from *The Black Americas: 1492–1992*. "The revolution did eliminate the visible, legal pillars of racism, and it seems to have enjoyed the support of poor blacks and mulattos."

GISELLE

Giselle Grau Garcells was born in the provincial city of Holguín in 1979. Following in the footsteps of her grandfather on her father's side, she began studying the piano at an early age. By the age of 10, she had won the first of many prizes, this one for best interpretation of Cuban music, at a music festival in the province of Las Tunas.

When I first met Giselle Grau, at a solo concert, she was 18 years old, had already performed in Mexico, Italy, and South America, and was an international prize winner. At her concert she played baroque and contemporary music with the same ease. I was seated next to a professional pianist, who was astounded by Giselle's professional serenity, effortless virtuosity, and above all, her ability to evoke the epic passion of complex compositions like Ginestera's Sonata No. 1.

Following the concert, I hesitated before going up to introduce myself to the pianist. I'd spoken to numerous performers, even those with a reputation for being "difficult," like Thelonious Monk, and never had a problem. But Giselle was a prodigy, and the prodigies I'd met before had usually been spoiled and arrogant.

I congratulated her on the concert and asked if I could meet with her for a longer interview. She had been the star of the evening. Usually, when I approached celebrities for an interview, I'd be asked to explain my intentions, to give a short history about the newspaper where I worked, and a number of other preliminaries.

"Please come and visit," she said. She smiled the way one does on the street with neighbors, with no sign of the self-satisfaction of being the center of attention. She jotted down her address and phone number in large, confident letters. It was a typical Cuban response, with

By age eighteen, Giselle Grau had played solo piano concerts on three continents, winning awards at home and abroad.

immediate trust of the stranger neutralizing even the most legitimate feelings of apprehension.

I watched her respond to other well-wishers. Her modesty came so naturally that I wondered if she would ever learn to bask in glory. Was this a young person who simply did not realize the magnitude of her accomplishments, or was she so mature in her simple but elegant dress that nothing fazed her.

In Havana, Giselle Grau lives with her uncle and aunt, where she can be close to the National School of Music and study with the great classical and jazz pianist Andrés Alén. Her uncle Julio insisted on going to meet me at my residence and walking me to his house.

My first surprise was to see Giselle informally dressed as I greeted her with a handshake. Curled up on the sofa, she looked ten years younger than she did at the concert, like anyone's teen-aged daughter. The second surprise was to hear her talk. She sounded as mature as her interpretation of Schumann and Lecuona.

"In the beginning I studied very little," she said. "But it was not out of rebelliousness. I began to take it seriously when I was fourteen."

That was the year she'd won a trip to Italy. But with all her accomplishments, she'll only practice three or four hours a day, "because I intend to finish my regular studies."

"When there's a concert or contest, I'll practice seven or eight hours a day."

No matter how hard I tried, I could get no response that implied any sort of sacrifice, none of the self-aggrandizement that one usually hears from people who work very hard to earn their laurels. What made it worth the toil for Giselle seemed to have little to do with the glory. In fact, there is no celebrity industry in Cuba. Professionals and artists are expected to be like everyone else, receiving a few extra perks for remaining among the faithful.

Giselle seemed to fit in the mold. She spoke more enthusiastically about her joy of music than her personal goals. "There's no one period I favor," she said. "I can find something exciting in most composers and all periods. I'm charmed by Bach, but I also love Samuel Barber. You have to make a sacrifice to play some of his works, and it's worth it."

I looked around the living room for signs of privilege in Giselle's Old Havana residence. The street outside was in typical disrepair. Inside, the walls needed painting. It was more spacious than other Old Havana apartments I'd visited. The living room chairs were generically old but comfortable. The paintings on the wall, representational art with a touch of abstraction, were interesting but not collector's items.

"We thought we had an original that might have been valuable," said Julio, pointing to one of the paintings, "but it turned out to be nothing special. But we like it."

The only suggestion of privilege in the whole living room was a Sharp fax machine, the same basic model I used at my home. What the family had not accumulated in material possessions was compensated for by culture. Julio had studied three careers at different points in his life: diplomacy, literature, and a technical field. With a commercial elite still lacking in Cuba, a cultural elite had emerged, including scientists, artists, and scholars, and Julio fit in perfectly.

"Those people you see out there hustling in the street," he said, "could have studied anything they liked, and for free. If they chose not to study, it's their decision."

Lourdes, Giselle's blond aunt, served me a cup of rich Cuban coffee.

A month before this interview, pitcher Liván Hernández had been named the most valuable player in baseball's World Series. He'd guided his Miami team to the championship. Hernández had earned about $10 a month on Cuba's national baseball team until he'd defected to the United States where he's earning millions.

"We don't blame Liván," Julio said. "Sartre writes about man's liberty to choose. Liván made a philosophical decision. Over here he was an anonymous hero."

"We had the choice of leaving with my father in 1960," said Lourdes. "We could have left but the idea never occurred to us. We only expect that those who leave should send back a percentage of what they earn to help the country. It's not Liván's leaving that bothers us. It's the way he did it."

I was happy that Giselle's uncle and aunt brought up the question of leaving one's country. Giselle had the talent to earn a comfortable living abroad, and I'd wanted to ask her if she'd ever thought of the idea. What would she do if she received a generous offer on one of her trips to remain abroad.

"Giselle," said Julio. "Be honest with your answer. Remember that you have the freedom to choose your destiny. Whatever you choose in your life, you would do so with our blessings."

Giselle seemed far removed from the ideological implications of the discussion.

"I'd love to receive a scholarship to study abroad," she said. "But that would be temporary. I like it here."

Her response was too vague, so I asked her to be more specific about what she liked.

"When I've gone to perform in other countries," she said, "I was distressed to meet so many musicians who had to study other careers and play music on the side. Music was not considered a profession in their countries, and so they couldn't develop themselves professionally the way I can here."

"That shocked me," Giselle continued. "They did not call music their career. Here in Cuba, music or the arts in general is considered a career, just as legitimate as being an engineer or a doctor."

"Here the arts are accessible to everyone," added Julio. "I know in some countries, most people cannot afford to hear a symphony orchestra. Here, there are symphonic concerts every Sunday and they only cost five Cuban pesos (about US 20 cents)." "In spite of all our hardships these days," he continued, "we have not allowed culture to be sacrificed."

Without knowing it, Giselle Grau was a part of Cuba's cultural elite. Her total nonchalance about her professional achievements reflected a remarkable indifference to celebrityhood. The music itself, and not the glories it promised, was her sole ambition.

During most interviews, the star elaborates on his or her accomplishments and then hopes the interview will end so he can get back to his business or pleasure. Giselle Grau Garcells was relaxing deep in the sofa, enjoying the conversation, with no rush for it to end.

GRINGO CHILD MEETS FIDEL

Erik Didonna was a New York boy in Cuba. Most foreign parents in Latin America send their children to private schools. But Cuba did not have private schools, so Erik's father, a film maker doing an historical documentary on Haitian immigration to Cuba, sent Erik to a Cuban public school from kindergarten through the third grade, between 1982 and 1985. Erik also returned to Cuba in 1988 for an extended vacation at the age of twelve.

"I had in my mind that Fidel was a hero," Erik said when I met him in 1997. "But many of my friends had nasty things to say about him. One friend said, 'I go to Miami or I die'. It was shocking. They said in different ways that Fidel wasn't a standup guy.

"But two girls I played with felt differently. Their father was a Chilean film maker who had left Chile for political reasons. After hearing my other friends talk badly about Fidel, the Chilean friends told me they were crazy about him. For them, Cuba meant freedom from Pinochet, so I could see how they might love him.

"I admire him as a leader. He went into the country and there was Batista who kept the rich in power. It was a great revolution with a purpose and Fidel actually had the courage to stand up to the Americans who wanted to stick their hands in there. In essence, Fidel beat them. He managed to make the country survive for 30 years. They're not unhealthy. They've got excellent schooling. They've got the best film industry in Latin America. State of the art. It's a good

109

thing that they invest money in culture to produce quality products. I love their animated hero, Elpidio Valdés, a revolutionary from the Spanish–Cuban war.

"So what went wrong? The blockade is definitely a factor, as well as the fact that socialism just doesn't work. It's good in theory but you can't put it into practice.

"You ask me about culture contrasts? Cubans are very jovial and full of life. The place is bursting with life. In comparison, in New York, where I'm from, there's a robotic state of mind. Cuba is warm and inviting as soon as you step off the plane. In New York there are places you just don't walk through. I don't know places like that in Cuba.

"In Cuba I was this rich kid. My friends were all poor. I didn't care. I saw them as equals. They never asked me for anything. I never met a Cuban who asked me for something. Cubans never lose their pride.

"I was a child when I met Fidel for the first time. He picked me up and I tugged at his beard."

And who's this guy? I asked.

This is Fidel, he answers. *In a few years you'll know me well.*

"A year or two later, still a child, I knew who Fidel was when I saw him at a reception. This time I went up to him."

Remember me? I asked.

He looked down.

No, I don't.

I told him who I was. *Of course you don't remember me. You must see five million kids every day!*, I said.

Then, my father was looking for me and couldn't find me.

I had disappeared. He found me on the balcony fifteen minutes later, talking with Fidel. I was very young at the time. I've tried many times to remember what we talked about but I can only guess that Fidel must have been very intrigued by an American kid in Cuba.

JON AND TONY

Jon and Tony don't know each other, but both have made recent trips to Cuba that were written up in the *Chronicle of Higher Education*.

110

Both are trained scholars, and both broke social and political barriers by traveling to Cuba. Tony Mendoza is from the Cuban exile community, where it is frowned upon to help Cuba with tourist dollars. He went to Cuba on a sabbatical and shot 80 rolls of film. Jon Torgerson was part of a group of 175 Americans who traveled to Cuba in order to defy the travel ban in 1993. Since then he has taken groups of college students to Cuba on an annual credit course from Drake University in Iowa.

Both Tony Mendoza and Jon Torgerson have interviewed hundreds of people in Cuba. They should have a lot in common. Yet they see Cuba with a totally distinct vision. I have traveled in many countries throughout the world and lived for extended periods of time on several continents. From my personal experience, no place has inspired such profoundly contrary points of view as Cuba.

I've taken the literary license to juxtapose quotes from Tony and John. The conversation is imaginary but comes directly from the words and writings of these two individuals. How two thinking people can look at the same image and see two different things suggests that your trip to Cuba will be an existential one, with your own life experience coloring everything you see.

Tony: Passengers on the flight had warned me that I was going to find a ruined Havana, but what I saw still surprised me. The same old factories that had lined the airport road during the 1950s were still there. After 37 years of socialism, the buildings [Havana's architecture] seemed to be exact copies of the ruined monuments of Greece and Roma. Instant antiquity.

Jon: [With nostalgia in his voice] It reminded me a lot of what America was like in the fifties, except there were all the rainbow colors.

Tony: As long as Fidel is around, nothing will change.

Jon: Even though Fidel has been opposed to partnerships with foreign companies, the people discussed this and the Party Congress endorsed the plan.

Tony: [What about] the absence of most basic freedoms?

Jon: A just society is one which first provides social and economic conditions which are sufficient to implement civil and political equality. We in the United States generally focus on the latter. Thus, we condemn a society which denies freedom of the press with no corresponding word of praise for that same country when it increases its literacy rate from 50 to 95 percent or makes genuine progress towards eliminating poverty. I gave a paper on human rights at the University of Havana and got no flak at all. I was critical that Cuba emphasizes social and economic rights at the cost of civil rights.

Tony: [What economic rights?] Most Cubans work for the state, which pays an average salary of $8 a month. On that pay, it's not possible to eat two meals a day.

Jon: Some of my own students see a lot of poverty in Cuba. I don't. I think the people, compared to those in other Latin American countries, are doing quite well.

(Aside): At a 1987 Equal Employment Opportunities Commission hearing, presided over by the now U.S. Supreme Court justice Clarence Thomas, Jon Torgerson declared: "I'd rather be among the worst 10 percent in Cuba than the same bottom level in the United States because of Cuba's social support system. One way of judging a society is how it treats its least fortunate." Thomas got upset, and rifled off a letter to the National Endowment for the Humanities protesting Torgerson's part in a conference with NEH funding.

Tony: People look depressed, beaten down. They stare into the distance, as if in a trance, as they wait for buses or in endless food lines, or when they sit on the sea wall, staring intently toward the horizon, toward Miami. The liveliness, humor, wit, and energy that I have always associated with Cubans are mostly gone.

Jon: My students have many different opinions but they're really impressed with Cubans' sense of community, being able to do things without money. They're overwhelmed by the cultural wealth.

One day I will try to bring Jon and Tony together for a cup of rich Cuban coffee. After all, they do agree on one thing:

Jon: Americans should see Cuba for themselves, but their government won't let them.
Tony: The United States should eliminate travel restrictions to Cuba and let Americans go to Havana.

I hope Tony and Jon will read these pages and make a point of getting together. The discussion will be exciting.

Tony: Few people are happy with socialism, with the Revolution, with Fidel.
Jon: I think Cuba is a viable alternative model for developing countries.

113

Chapter Five

SOCIAL CUSTOMS: A TO Z

AFRICAN HERITAGE

More than a third of all Cubans are considered black, and most other Cubans, many of whom are mulattos, carry the African heritage within their spirit.

West Africa, in particular Nigeria, the Congo, Senegal, the Gambia, and Guinea, was the source of slaves brought in by the Spaniards. Most of these West Africans brought with them the Yoruba culture, whose Santería customs (see Religion in this chapter) survived the colonial period. Yoruba gods were hidden behind the faces of Catholic saints. Other Afro-Cubans migrated from Haiti and the Bahamas.

Some Cuban researchers believe that the naive frankness and freedom from repressive inhibitions of both blacks and whites in Cuba comes from the African cultural heritage. Curiously, Afro-Cuban music now influences the contemporary West African music scene. My former student Serge plays keyboard in a California-based Afro-Cuban music group called Máquina Loca, whose lead singer is from Nigeria.

Even though Afro-Cubans played a major role in history, as exemplified by independence leader Antonio Maceo, Batista, a mulatto, was not permitted to join the Havana Yacht Club. All forms of segregation were abolished by the revolution, and the country is now officially considered Afro-Cuban.

ARTS

In the absence of a commercial-business power structure, Cuba's arts community may have become the elite of the nation. Since 1959, Cuban officialdom has invested considerable resources into creating a truly national arts infrastructure, founding numerous schools in art, dance, and film. Cuba's Ballet Nacional, Conjunto de Danza Nacional, and Conjunto Folklórico Nacional are all acclaimed internationally, and the Cuban School of Ballet is recognized as one of the best in the world.

Afro-Cuban masks

115

Naive art is an important genre in Cuba today.

Cuban composers in various musical genres have won prizes abroad. Havana is the host of an exciting international jazz festival. (The international impact of Cuban music is great enough to warrant a separate discussion in this book — see Chapter Six).

A renaissance of sorts is taking place in painting and sculpture, with genres extending from art-naif to abstract, although a number of fine Cuban artists have chosen to leave the island and live abroad. Particularly exciting to this observer is the wealth of "naive art," many of whose practitioners have no formal training. Catch the permanent exhibit in Havana's El Morro fortress museum.

Cuba's premier art festival is the biannual Bienal de La Habana. Anything goes at this festival, as exemplified in 1997 by a work by the 27-year-old Kcho, a 20-foot-high sculpture cobbled together from frazzled ship remnants, suitcases, and old furniture, what one critic called "a calculatedly ambiguous reference to the country's boat emigrations."

A cadre of Cuban film directors, led by Tomás Gutiérrez Alea and Humberto Solás, have produced many more artistically-acclaimed films than should be imaginable for a country of only 11 million, and successful film makers from many different countries have studied film at Cuba's Escuela Internacional de Cine, TV y Video. Havana hosts the prestigious International Festival of Latin American Cinema.

As pianist Giselle Grau noted, artists in Cuba are not obligated to earn a living doing something else while practising their art on the side, although dissenters note that the politics of official recognition may stand in the way in the plastic arts and literature.

Travelers planning to visit Cuba can get a head start before they go by renting movies like *Fresa y Chocolate* and *Guantanamera*, by seeing color images of Cuban artists on the Internet, and by catching in-person performances by some of the many Cuban salsa and jazz groups that travel abroad regularly.

BASEBALL

Foreign visitors to Cuba may experience great culture shock when attending a game of baseball, a deceptively plodding confrontation between nine specialists on each team that erupts in explosively dramatic moments. It is ironic that the U.S. and Cuba have spent a large part of the second half of the twentieth century on less than friendly terms, for both countries share the same national pastime.

How did Cubans become so fanatic about a sport that seems so typical of the United States? Most Americans believe that baseball was exported to Cuba some time after the 1898 Spanish-American War. But Cubans were already playing the game at the end of Spain's colonial empire.

Evidence suggests that Cuba's pre-Hispanic Taino Indians played a game called *batey* that was remarkably similar to baseball. In 1869, Esteban Bellán went to study at Fordham University in New York and ended up playing baseball with a team called the Troy Haymakers. Bellán became the first Cuban athlete in U.S. professional baseball. In 1874, he returned to Cuba to organize a baseball league.

In the first half of the twentieth century, racially-integrated Cuban teams encountered diplomatic problems when arriving to play in segregated baseball leagues of the United States. Some black Cubans played in the old "Negro Leagues" in the United States.

Today, many Americans have become disenchanted with increasingly corporatized professional baseball. Millionaire players no longer maintain long-standing allegiance to a given team and its supporters, charge money for autographs, and leave their loyal fans behind in search of extra millions on other teams' larger markets. In this context, Cuban "defectors" to American baseball are not much different than a "free agent" who leaves the loyal fans of the Oakland As for a juicier contract with the New York Yankees.

In some ways, Cuba's national baseball league is a return to what baseball used to be, with each city's team having its loyal followers.

In some neighborhoods, Cubans actually play the informal stickball version of the sport, which for me brings back the nostalgia of my childhood on the streets of New York. Cuba's main baseball season runs from mid-November through March. Cuba's national team often wins the Gold Medal in Olympic competition. (Cuba also excels competitively in boxing, track and field, and volleyball.) During the Special Period, the government began authorizing Cuban baseball players to perform abroad in amateur leagues in order to earn hard currency for the country. The temporary loss of these players has had a negative impact on Cuba's performance in international tournaments.

It's easy to get tickets for Cuban baseball games. Just ask around in whichever city you may be. I won't succumb to temptations to explain the rules of this game in writing. If baseball is new for you, attend a game and ask the Cubans sitting near you to explain what is happening as it happens. You'll find that it's not so complicated.

CHINATOWN

Havana's Chinatown is today making a comeback. Following the revolution, most Chinese residents left Cuba. I met one of them in a Chinese restaurant in Chicago. I noticed he was speaking Spanish, and asked him where he'd learned the language.

"In the fifties, I left China to escape communism," he said. "I ended up in Cuba. But it looked like communism was following me around. After the revolution in Cuba, I left again, this time to Chicago."

Most of Cuba's Chinese are descendents of indentured servants, brought to the island in the nineteenth century to labor on plantations and build the railroads. Cuba's Chinatown, a few blocks west of the Capitolio in Centro Habana, seems small and almost insignificant, until you stroll in its pedestrian mall and eat in its restaurants. The food is tasty, and roving musicians add to the atmosphere.

Chinatown's open-air produce market is one of the best in Havana.

119

CIGARS

The marvels of Cuban tobacco were well-known to native Cubans long before the arrival of the Spaniards, who initially had mixed feelings about this natural wonder. Even the word "cigar" comes from an Indian language.

At one time, the colonial church banned the weed, until realizing that it was more advantageous to tax it. In 1717, the first Cuban rebellion against the Spaniards was in opposition to the tobacco tax.

Tobacco is a democratic crop in that it is best produced not on large plantations but on small farms where each plant receives personal care. Most tobacco workers were freemen rather than slaves. By the nineteenth century, Cuba's best tobacco was being produced in the Vuelta Abajo region of the western province of Pinar del Río.

Tobacco seedlings are planted, and then transplanted in November, conforming to the 80-to-90 day winter growing cycle, when the days are warm, the nights cool, and there is a minimum of rainfall. After the March harvest, leaves are sorted and left to dry for about a month and a half in a *casa de tabaco*.

Once dried, the leaves are subjected to a fermentation process. Most good cigars are double-fermented. Cohibas are fermented three times. This composting mellows the flavor of the leaf and lowers the already low tar and nicotine content of the unique Cuban leaves.

Some leaves grow covered from the sunlight by large cheesecloth tents that filter in a minimal amount of sunlight and wind. These leaves are used as the *capa*, or wrapper, of the finest cigars.

(If you smoke cigarettes, you're getting the leaves that were rejected by cigar producers.)

Rolling cigars is not easy and it can take as long as ten months for a newcomer to become adept at producing the simplest shapes. Traditionally, workers were provided entertainment by a *lector*, who read the daily newspaper in the morning and other literature during the afternoon.

Cubans and cigar lovers around the world will disagree as to which are the best cigars, and this is a matter of taste. Cohibas are generally the "favorites," but underdog lovers say they're not as good as they used to be, and prefer Montecristo, Partagas, Romeo y Julieta, H. Upmann (John F. Kennedy's favorites), Hoyo de Monterrey, or others.

Once you have a reputable brand, a good choice of cigar may have more to do with its size and shape than the brand itself. The fuller-flavored large sizes (*corona*) or the short but stout *robustos* are two preferred shapes, and smaller, thinner cigars are too hot-burning for some aficionados.

Travelers with a limited budget who choose to buy from a street seller should make sure the box is sealed and has official marks. The salesman should then open the cedar box so that the buyer can see that the cigars are all the same size and shape.

To smoke, snip off just enough of the tip to give a good draw and do not inhale.

Cigars are best kept in humidors lined with cedar that maintain the humidity at about 71 percent.

COMMUNITY

Many Americans who delve deeply into the Cuban way of life are particularly surprised at the sense of community, while Europeans from more traditional settings will be less perplexed.

U.S. political exile Assata Shakur says that "being in Cuba has allowed me to live in a society that is not at war with itself. There is a sense of community. It is a given in Cuba that if you fall down, the person next to you is going to help you get up."

Health educator Gina Margillo believes that sense of community contributes to the long life expectancy of Cubans by providing an emotional support system. Cuba may one day become a part of the "global village," but the local neighborhood will remain the nucleus of Cuban social life.

CORRUPTION?

"Someone said that no Cuban steals a million pesos but that a million Cubans steal one peso each day," wrote Havana resident and independent Internet journalist Miguel Fernández Martínez, in "Illegal Lives."

"It's the necessity of survival that has forced this people to assume a posture of illegality as a rational means of living."

Fernández's view is from the bottom up. John Kavulich, president of the U.S.–Cuba Trade and Economic Council and probably the person who has studied the Cuban business scene better than any other living foreigner, has a top-down perspective. His non-profit organization is the best source of information on doing business in Cuba.

Kavulich told me that business deals may involve inviting Cubans to dinner or giving a bottle of rum as a gift, typical in business dealings around the world.

"Every once in awhile, and it's extremely rare, do you hear of any business person making a payoff, and that's one in a thousand."

After having lived in both Mexico and Bolivia, where most business deals involved some sort of bribe, I find the comparative lack of corruption in Cuba remarkable and refreshing. But will it remain this way as Cuba enters the global economy?

DOING BUSINESS

The rules for doing business in Cuba are evolving on a daily basis and will continue to be modified during the next decade. This is the bad news. The good news is that you won't have to bribe anyone to get things going. Here are a few tips that will make your Cuban business experience a positive and profitable one. Foreigners doing business in Cuba must have a partner. In fact, they all have the same partner: the government, in what is called *empresa mixta* (literally: mixed enterprise, but similar to joint venture). The number of joint ventures increased from 20 in 1991 to more than 260 at the end of 1996.

But with such rumbling effervescence in the business arena, no one rules out the possibility that foreigners may be allowed exclusive proprietorship of certain enterprises. On the other hand, if class divisions in Cuban society become aggravated as capitalism extends to more remote stations, whichever government is in power could also step in and stop the train.

With United States corporations out of contention during the trade embargo, Cuba's idiosyncratic business scenario has been unlike that of the rest of Latin America. Enterprises from more than 30 countries are having a much better chance to succeed than they would in neighboring Mexico, for example, with NAFTA (North American Free Trade Act) competition. The number of foreign companies registering trademarks in Cuba is increasing at a spectacular rate.

By 1977, the United States Department of Commerce was aware that other countries had gotten the jump. The DOC then stepped in to allow certain U.S. corporations loophole permits to begin making waves on the shore of the Malecón, sidestepping the embargo legislation with remarkable legal agility.

The probabilities of your business being approved by the Cuban government greatly increase if you enter negotiations armed with evidence that your enterprise will provide social benefits for the Cuban population.

For the time being, this does not mean paying high salaries. The Cuban government will determine the salaries you pay, in accordance with its desperate attempt to maintain social equality. Depending on the source you read, the ratio between the lowest and highest salary is between 4:1 and 7:1, which makes Cuba, on paper at least, the most equitable society in Latin America.

As has been noted, with the separate dollar economy, Cubans without access to dollars are considerably more vulnerable to the tribulations of inequality than salary differentials seem to indicate. Tips earned by workers within the tourist industry give them more economic leverage than salary differentials would indicate.

Cuba's first income tax is now approved, with a double purpose of increasing state revenue and restoring economic equality by targeting dollar earners only. Tax collecting in other Latin American countries is quite haphazard, as contributors to political campaigns find a myriad of loopholes and governments lack the political will to do anything about it. But Cuba may be more earnest in this endeavor, as Fidel Castro and other government officials who struggle to maintain social equality remain reticent about the role of foreign business interests.

Cuba's involvement with foreign investment has been called "dancing with the devil" and more than a few officials dislike the emergence of the new rich. "None of us sheds a tear because there are no millionaires in Cuba," said Fidel Castro.

So the greatest burden upon any foreign entrepreneur is to show tangible proof to Cuban society that the enterprise is benefiting the nation by creating new jobs, by paying taxes faithfully, and by expanding the economy. Since the Cuban government is a full partner with foreign companies, once initial foreign investments are paid off, the 50 percent of the profits belonging to the governmental partner are directed toward social benefits like subsidized food, free education and health care, and accessibility of cultural activities to all Cubans.

"Profits are divided equally between the outside entrepreneurs and Cuban shareholders, our people," said Marcos Portal Leon, Cuba's Minister of Basic Industry. "The half that goes outside the country is taxed," he added, "but at amenable rates."

I spoke with one foreign entrepreneur who was pained by the fact that he couldn't pay higher salaries and resorted to less tangible perks and fringe benefits for his employees. At one joint-venture restaurant chain, employees actually make as much as two hundred dollars a month (ten times as much as a physician) by sharing the 10-percent gratuity that is included in the meal prices.

Entrepreneurs sensitive to environmental concerns will also be well received. Experienced organic food producers as well as manu-facturers who can operate with reduced energy may find a significant opening.

"We're particularly open to oil exploration and mining compa-nies, as well as new tourist facilities," said Minister Portal Leon. But given how easy it is to get a hotel room in Cuba, and with more hotels scaling above the Havana skyline, this author sees a potential glut in tourist facilities. Other observers respond that a post-embargo Cuba may need every hotel room it can get, with a sudden wave of tourists from the United States.

Given the bizarre business and social scenarios of this transition period in Cuban history, it is possible for a foreign entrepreneur to make money and be a humanitarian at the same time. According to *Canadian Business* (Oct 10, 1997), York Medical Inc. of Canada is licensing and marketing Cuban products to major drug and medical-device manufacturers. CEO David Allan "extols the humanitarian virtues of his partnership with the Cuban government."

"Canada has become a catalyst for Cuba's economic rehabilita-tion," according to a *Maclean's* article of November 3, 1997, and one wonders which is the greater motivation in Canada's fervent involvement in Cuba: a desire for substantial business profits or a resentment at what Canadians have considered U.S. heavy-handedness.

Embargo or no embargo, United States corporations are not about to stand by idly and watch a business bonanza of Canadians, Mexicans, Spaniards, and other foreigners. A New York-based non-profit organization called the U.S.–Cuba Trade and Economic Council gathers every iota of information, legal and financial, that can help U.S. businesses waiting in the wings.

John Kavulich, president of the organization, told this writer that the one thing everyone should know about Cuba's business situation is that it is changing on a daily basis.

"Anything that's prohibited today may be allowed tomorrow," Kavulich said, "and anything allowed today might be prohibited tomorrow."

Business people who thrive on uncertainty will fall deeply in love with Cuba.

FESTIVALS

In Latin America, even the most hedonistic festivals usually have some connection with Catholic traditions. With religious glasnost and the subsequent visit of the Pope, expect some religious traditions to make a mild comeback, but Cuba remains the most secular of all Latin American countries and most annual events do not involve a religious ceremony.

Any end-of-century list of annual events needs to be marked with an asterisk, as the Special Period has curtailed the scheduling of some of these events.

Some of the many annual events will be outlined here, but remember that *joie de vivre* is an inherent part of the Cuban culture and Cubans do not need an annual event to erupt into festivities.

Since festival dates are often changed, and many events are bi-annual, an outline of Cuban events cannot be in chronological order.

For example, the every-other-year Havana International Jazz Festival, once a February event, was moved up to mid-December in 1987.

Cuba is also the site of a profusion of international professional conferences. The best source for annual and bi-annual festival and professional conference dates is your nearest travel agency specializing in Cuba. (See phone/fax numbers and addresses in the Cuba Crib Sheet at the end of this book.)

Carnaval

The Yoruba cultural heritage of Cuba's carnival, called Carnaval, is quite similar to that of Brazil's Carnaval or Mardi Gras in New Orleans. But Cuba's Carnaval, centered in the city with its most extensive African heritage, Santiago, is celebrated in late July and the beginning of August rather than during the period leading up to Lent.

Carnaval originally celebrated the end of the sugar harvest, when slaves were allowed to escape their oppressive existence for a week. Coinciding in both date and place is the anniversary of the daring July 26, 1953 assault on the barracks of Moncada by the opposition movement, led by Castro. A pre-Lent version of Carnaval is held on weekend evenings in February in front of the Capitolio in Havana.

Carnaval originated in the Yoruban custom of singing praise to the saints. Each *orisha* had a particular conga or rumba dance rhythm. Throughout Latin America, Carnaval dancing groups are called *comparsas*, and are accompanied by drummers, singers, and trumpets.

Daily processions are led by dancers dressed in traditional costumes from slave days. Rumba and rum flow freely and dancing gets more intense as the night hours drift toward morning.

For several years during the Special Period, no Carnaval was held, but as the economic situation was picking up, Carnaval was renewed in 1997.

Havana Events

The **Havana International Jazz Festival** is one of the top highlights for international visitors, and as hard times mellow out, this bi-annual event is one of the most-likely festivals to become an annual affair. Jazz delegations come from all around the world to rediscover that rhythmic and harmonic innovations in Cuba are among the most daring and exciting in the world of jazz. Hear cool and hot jazz at the festival, usually during Havana's coolest weather, and often held in December.

Ever since Dizzy Gillespie, Cal Tjader, and Herbie Mann brought Cuban music to an international audience, jazz musicians have been enriching their rhythms and nuances by taking in the Cuban jazz experience. This author's personal favorites in Cuban jazz are the group Irakere (which has influenced Cuban popular music) and the virtuoso pianist Gonzalo Rubalcaba.

Some of the other bi-annual festivals held in Havana, with approximate months, are: the International Guitar Festival (May), the International Theatre Festival (August or September), the Interna-

Photo: Siomara Cramer

Havana street festival: joy and racial harmony during hard times.

tional Ballet Festival (October), and the International Festival of Latin American Film (December). Cuba's outstanding accomplishments in both ballet and film are recognized around the world.

An impressive list of fairs, expositions, and scientific and cultural *congresos* would occupy a whole booklet. Whatever one's academic specialty may be, Havana or other parts of Cuba will certainly offer a symposium in the field.

Santiago's Festivities

Cuba's "second city" is most known for the Carnaval, but Santiago is host to other important events. Those interested in seeing music, song, and dance in the context of other Caribbean cultures should enjoy the annual **Festival of Caribbean Culture** in either June or July. Following the August Carnaval, the tempo slows down for a festival of romantic *bolero*. In much of Latin America, romantic music is making a comeback after years of being considered passé, but romantic music never died in Cuba. In the cooler month of December, the **International Choir Festival** is held.

In Camagüey

Cuba's third-largest city has its own Carnaval in steamy August, but the most regional of Camagüey celebrations is **Jornadas de la Cultura Camagüeyana**, usually in the comfortable weeks of early February. Cuba's national poet, Nicolás Guillén, was born in Camagüey, and the house of his birth is open to the public.

Holguín

At last we come to a more typical Latin American pilgrimage with the **Romería de Mayo**. Pilgrims arrive during the first week in May to ascend the Loma de la Cruz and visit a cross that was placed at the top by the Spaniards at the end of the eighteenth century to ward off drought. Outdoor musicians greet the pilgrims in town plazas.

The more secular **Fiesta Iberoamericana de Cultura** with its street fairs, theater, and dance, is celebrated in October. The dance gets more serious in November with the bi-annual **International Ballet Festival**.

Trinidad

Colonial Trinidad is the ideal setting for festivals, and between events, visitors can choose among an array of museums, from sacred Catholic and African to colonial and modern history. Nineteenth century romanticism is featured in Casa Cantero and Museo Romántico.

The **Fiestas Sanjuaneras** is a Cuban take on the Day of San Juan, celebrated throughout the Hispanic world around the time of the summer solstice in June. In late November, the **Semana de la Cultura Trinitaria** maintains a regional tenor, while so many other Cuban festivals have been internationalized.

Matanzas

Many of Cuba's internationally-recognized rumba groups have come out of Matanzas. The Afro-urban rumba (music and dance rhythms) is one of Cuba's most complex and electrifying contributions to the international culture scene. Beginning October 10 and lasting for a week and a half is the **Festival del Bailador Rumbero**, at the impressive 1862 neo-classical Teatro Santo.

Remedios (Province of Villa Clara)

The town of Remedios, with a population of about 20,000, is one of Cuba's most attractive colonial towns and remains off the tourist trail. Christmas has not been a major festival in Cuba, but at the same time (December 24–26), this seventeenth-century town and neighboring villages celebrate **Las Parrandas,** a competition to see which neighborhood produces the best *carroza* (float). A spirit of controlled chaos, with street music and dancing, country fair goods on sale, and fireworks, is the vestige of year-end religious celebrations from the 1800s.

FOOD

Marta, from Colombia, is a film student at Cuba's prestigious film school in San Antonio de los Baños.

"My greatest culture shock was the lack of balance in the diet," Marta says. "At the school cafeteria, sometimes they give us a breakfast with no bread, and then we are served a lunch with mainly starch and yet with a whole lot of bread. That's just an example."

According to Cuban researchers Pérez and Muñoz in *Agricultura y Alimentación en Cuba*, the culturally acceptable diet is one that is both unhealthy (high-calorie, high-fat, high-cholesterol, low-fiber) and expensive to obtain, in that much of the food and the materials to produce it must be imported.

"Food surveys in Cuba," cite agricultural scientists Rosset and Benjamin from Pérez and Muñoz, show that what Cubans want for both lunch and dinner, every day, is rice, beans, a high-protein food (such as beef, poultry, pork, fish, and eggs), *viandas* (which in order of preference are plantains, taro, potatoes, cassava [what we know as *yuca*], and sweet potato), and bread."

Cuba's colonial legacy, which was continued during the U.S. and Soviet periods, was that of importing *criollo* foods "neither well-suited to Cuban agriculture nor particularly healthy."

The long-term effects of the Special Period may actually be beneficial to Cuba's eating habits. Cuban agronomists are well-aware that beef production is far more costly and inefficient than using the same resources to grow *viandas*, fruit, vegetables, and even to produce pork meat.

Pigs need considerably less terrain than cattle and willingly eat municipal refuse rather than expensive grain. In the United States, this author once raised pigs on a diet of 90 percent municipal refuse and used the rest of the available land that would have been occupied by cattle to grow fruit and vegetables.

During the 1990s, Cuba's government sustained a policy that encouraged the substitution of *viandas* and vegetables for wheat and

131

rice, also substituting vegetable for animal fat. Can Cubans voluntarily change their eating habits?

I did dine with some Cubans who particularly enjoyed a tasty salad with avocado, cucumber, and tomato, and I actually found one young lady who claimed she preferred a vegetarian diet. Her preferred *congris* (rice with beans), an excellent non-animal source of protein, is comprised of staples that are not traditionally grown natively.

Food preference is so much a matter of taste and culture that I can only relate the highs and lows of eating in Cuba from a perspective slanted by my personal taste.

Lows: fiberless white bread, fats used in food preparation that may sometimes be lard (the government encourages the use of vegetable oil, which was not always available), hotel food in general, lack of variety, and absence of hot sauces. Lobster and other sea delights have not been fished sustainably and the supply is dwindling because of exports and overuse in tourist hotels. All of my eating has been with Cubans, so I have not had much of an opportunity to eat sea food.

Highs: avocados and cucumbers, as fresh and tasty as anywhere in the world; pork, prepared with bitter orange and garlic, or the juicy crispy *lechón* (roasted pig); the rice with bean dish *congris*, which in combination with salad and fruit is a complete vegetarian meal; the root *yuca* cooked with garlic; fried bananas (I'm afraid to ask what they fry them in); the unbelievably tasty home-cooked food and personal service at the small family eating places called *paladares*, most of them in people's homes with a funky *ambiente*; the eating experience in Chinatown; the open air fruit and vegetable markets; boxed natural fruit drinks called Tropical Island.

FRANKNESS

Let the anecdotes and compiled experiences in this book from both Cubans and foreign visitors be entered in evidence that frankness is a fundamental characteristic among most Cubans.

Having lived among New Yorkers, who have made an art form of bluntness, I sense that the Cuban penchant for calling things as they are is less brash and more naive than the New York brand, more stylized, and often tinged with nuances of sly humor.

MACHISMO?

For three decades, Cuban film makers have been producing movies that encouraged women to become independent. Thanks to food rationing and free health care, women have found less of a need to be dependent on men. With basic necessities assured and equal access to professions, a Cuban woman is much less likely to remain in a bad marriage out of economic necessity, as many of her unfortunate counterparts in other Latin countries do.

Lucía was the first post-1959 film to ridicule the institution of *machismo* (male dominance). In the third of the film's three related stories, a man risks being ostracized by the whole neighborhood when he balks at allowing his wife Lucía to participate in evening theater activities. Enjoying the support of her neighbors, Lucía defies her husband. Decades before *Mr. Mom*, Lucía's husband was obligated to deal with domestic and child-raising duties traditionally reserved for women.

"But machismo still exists," says Melania, a young woman from the colonial city of Trinidad. "A Cuban woman will split as soon as she finds out her man is not supportive or faithful. All Cuban men chase after women," she adds, smiling and pointing at her husband Nufo.

"That's not true, and you know it!" responds Nufo.

Is Nufo faithful? It's hard to tell because it's not socially acceptable among men to admit that they don't play around on the side. But at least Nufo is not embarrassed to change a diaper.

Many Cuban women think preventively, preferring to live with a man without formal vows, at least until their partner's loyalty is proven.

To what extent does machismo, the Latin form of male dominance, still exist in Cuba? I've asked this question several times in groups of Cubans. My inquiry always provokes a lively debate. The consensus has been "yes, it still exists, but not nearly as much as it used to."

In most of Latin America, male literacy statistics are superior to women's, by more than a few percentage points. In Cuba, male and female literacy are the same. There are as many women doctors as there are men. Machismo may still exist, but the Cuban woman has been given the educational and economic tools to find her own fulfillment, independent of traditional domestic obligations, should she choose that route.

MOJITO

The *mojito* is one of Cuba's distinctive mixed drinks, and a favorite of many foreign visitors. Even people who don't like the hard stuff will wonder how this blend goes down so mellow. Mix a shot of rum with: a half teaspoon of sugar, squeezed juice from half of a large lime, soda water, ice, and the key ingredient, yerbabuena, a pungent herb from the mint family with medicinal properties. Yerbabuena is a Latin American herb that has gained favor in international food stores around the world. Some people prefer to squeeze the yerbabuena as they deposit it in the glass in order to release its flavor.

PERSONAL HYGIENE

In tropical Cuba, informal dress is the rule, but don't let that mislead you. Cubans are extremely fastidious about cleanliness and manage to look well-dressed even with the simplest of clothing.

Writing about post-Soviet hardships, Oppenheimer noted that food scarcity "was not what seemed to bother Cubans the most. What people seemed most irked about was the shortage of soap, deodorant, shampoo, toothpaste, shaving cream and perfume."

PRIVACY

Forget it. If you come from a culture that values privacy, you'd better begin changing your ways before you come to Cuba.

Out on the street I was greeted by a young man outside an elementary school. He was waiting to pick up his daughter.

"I noticed you're staying in the Hotel Caribbean," he said. "How much do you pay there?"

Pretty brash for a stranger. In my country, my response would be automatic. None of your business, I'd say. But in any Cuban neighborhood, where everyone knows everyone else, you are expected to be frank.

"It's twenty a night," I said.

"Well, in case you leave the hotel, I know a woman who charges ten for a room in her house. Where are you from?"

Etcetera.

135

In Old Havana I stopped at a restaurant to check out the menu at the entrance. Two young women came out from behind the menu board.

"What are you looking at?" asked the one dressed in a tight spandex outfit, yellow-and-black striped, that reminded me of a yellow jacket. I remembered that yellow jackets don't sting unless provoked.

"Just checking out the menu."

"Where are you from?" the same woman asked.

"Originally from the U.S.," I said, "but most of the time I've lived in Bolivia."

The Bolivia answer was both true and convenient. When people discovered I was based in the second-poorest country in the hemisphere, they were less likely to see me as a wealthy tourist.

"Where are you headed," the yellow jacket asked.

"Just strolling," I said.

I must have looked reluctant. I was still not totally accustomed to being addressed by strangers with questions that in my culture come from friends or acquaintances.

"*No tengas miedo*" (don't worry) was the typical response. "We don't want anything. We just like to chat. Why don't you walk with us for awhile?"

Cubans have learned that people from more private cultures are sometimes taken aback by their openness, which verges on aggressiveness. The *No tengas miedo* almost says "Hey, why are you so suspicious of people who like to chat?"

Personally I'm not bothered by the probing, not when I compare its antithesis: the anonymity of American suburbia, where if you don't belong to a formal club or "support group," you could live there for years without getting to know anyone. Given a choice between the two extremes, I now prefer being the object of the Cuban candid camera over the standoffish privacy of North American suburbia.

This old Havana street usually bustles with people, but early Sunday morning is the best moment for some solitude.

Perhaps in the mountains among the more reserved *guajira* country people, you might get away with sitting in a corner for a moment of solitude and contemplation. But even the traditional *guajira* music is socially interactive, as singers engage in lyrical duels with improvised personal jabs.

PUBLIC GOOD VERSUS INDIVIDUAL RIGHTS

The one custom most apt to cause a case of culture shock among visitors from Western countries is Cuba's stance regarding the public good. In issues where public good enters in conflict with individual rights, Cubans opt for public good. There is no constitutional right in Cuba, for example, for citizens to own firearms. Individual ownership of guns is against the law. Cubans point to statistics on high murder rates by armed aggressors in the United States as an example of how certain individual rights can harm the public good.

One telling illustration is Cuba's policy for deterring the spread of AIDS. Cuba's first known case of AIDS in 1985 came with a heterosexual soldier returning from Mozambique. The disease later spread to homosexuals.

In the United States, gay and civil liberties activists did everything they could to prevent the stigma of AIDS from leading to job dismissals and housing discrimination. The fear of insurance companies dropping coverage for HIV-positive clients was another civil rights issue that influenced public policy on AIDS. These were real fears, as anti-gay sentiment was on the rise.

Fears of infringements on civil liberties caused public health officials in the United States to refrain from applying standard public health disease-containment measures of routine testing of at-risk individuals, even though such individuals would have the right to refuse testing. Also prevented was full-scale confidential reporting; an aggressive attempt to get notification of sexual partners of HIV-positive patients to health authorities was hampered by the individual rights issue.

According to reporter Chandler Burr, "the gay community decided that the disease hurt homosexuals vulnerable to a hostile society at least as much by pitilessly outing them as it did by killing them."

Some organizations defending the individual rights of HIV and AIDS victims warned policy makers that the government could use the virus as an excuse to conduct a new holocaust. The dangerous example they highlighted was Cuba. Cuba was vulnerable to such criticism because of her former policy of social and professional ostracism of homosexuals, a theme explored critically in the prize-winning film *Fresa y Chocolate*.

"Cuba has been notorious for its draconian treatment of people infected with the virus that causes AIDS," wrote Juanita Darling in the *Los Angeles Times* (July 24, 1997). "The government has rounded up everyone infected with the human immunodeficiency virus and locked them up in sanitoriums until they developed AIDS and died."

Instead of such draconian measures, many Western countries resorted to sex education, condoms, and needle exchange, teaching people how to act with care.

Stories of concentration camps in Cuba for HIV-positive citizens were bandied about without much documentation. In order to set things straight, Cuba sponsored a public conference on its AIDS policy on August 7, 1997. Jorge Pérez, director of Cuba's Pedro Kouri Institute of Tropical Medicine and most responsible for "the most hated AIDS program in the world," was the main speaker.

The statistics Dr. Pérez gave to the audience were confirmed independently by the World Health Organization. Per capita there were 35 times more deaths from AIDS in the United States than in Cuba. The most recent figures from 1993 showed that there were 276 new cases of AIDS per million in the United States. Cuba had only 7 per million. Puerto Rico, a Caribbean territory under the U.S. public health system but culturally similar to Cuba, had 654 new cases per million.

But had human rights been trampled to attain these impressive statistics? Was this the classic case of Mussolini getting the trains to run on time?

Delegates to the conference were taken to Cuba's largest sanatorium, Santiago de las Vegas. It was discovered that people with AIDS could choose to stay in or leave the sanatorium. Most choose to stay, since the medical care is superb and they receive 3,500 calories a day in food, much more than the rest of the population was receiving during the Special Period.

Cuba's public health statistics in other realms are equally impressive as its AIDS record, and this comes without economic incentives for its leading professionals. Cuba's chief epidemiologist at the Department of Public Health earned US $23 per month at the time of the conference.

Dr. Pérez asked the delegates for more cooperation from outside Cuba. "I want to make people understand," he said, "how damaging the blockade is to our ability to control the AIDS epidemic, to our getting publications, data, research, and medicines."

Lots of excitement in front of the Cathedral of Havana, but not much happening inside. This may change after the Pope's recent visit.

In controlling the spread of AIDS better than any other country in the world, Cuba has used traditional methods of thorough testing, reporting, and notification to an extent that may be considered intrusive by civil libertarians, with a sanatorium system that causes advocates of freedom in Western democracies to recoil with culture shock.

"What's different in Cuba," writes author and former AIDS reporter Elinor Burkett, "is that people don't think about individual rights. Most Americans think that when we're balancing social good and individual rights, we err toward the latter. Cubans are trained in the opposite mentality, so my friends in the sanitoriums believe there's a social good coming out of it."

RELIGION

Cuba is the least Catholic of all the Latin American countries, although this may change in the years following the January 1998 visit of the Pope. Why Catholicism is less evident in Cuba is open to speculation. Even before Castro closed all private schools, including those run by churches, and instituted a total separation of church and state, only about 10 percent of Cubans attended church regularly. By 1997, according to Jesuit visitor Raymond A. Schroth, that figure was less than 2 percent.

Father José Felix, a Cuban church leader, said: "I have young people coming to my parish who are curious about Catholicism. But they don't even know who Jesus Christ is."

Historically, the Catholic Church was part of the Spanish colonial regime. In Cuba, colonialism lasted four decades longer than in most other Latin American countries, and with the Catholic Church as an integral part of the colonial system, some Cubans still associate the Church with abuses of the past.

In nearby Mexico, village priests led the independence movement. But in Cuba, independence insurgents were mostly secular.

As the most oppressed sector of Cuban colonial society, blacks could be expected to identify with the underdog. In religion, the underdog was Santería, the Afro-Cuban faith with origins in the Yoruba culture of west Africa, as well as other west African creeds.

"Because Christian slave owners in the New World forbade the practice of pagan religions," according to historian Mark Kurlansky, "followers disguised the *orishas* [African Gods and Goddesses] as Christian saints."

"Santería insiders calculated that there were as many as four thousand *Babalaos* [Santería priests, also *babalawos*] in Cuba," wrote Oppenheimer. "In comparison, there were only two hundred fifty Roman Catholic priests in Cuba," this in the early 1990s.

Although religious belief was always tolerated during the revolutionary period, organized religion was frowned upon, and regular church goers might find it more difficult to get ahead in their professions. But the *babalawos*, who practice out of their homes, were less restricted than Catholic priests.

In November 1991, the Cuban Communist Party repealed the ban on organized religion and invited religious believers to join the party. In 1992, the Marxist-Leninist definition of the Cuban state was removed from the constitution, further opening the doors to religion.

Even before the Pope's visit, Catholicism was undergoing a renewal of sorts. The Church became an accepted conduit for charitable donations from abroad during the post-Soviet period, and international Catholic organizations such as Catholic Relief Services escalated their aid programs.

"Baptisms increased from seven thousand in 1971 to more than thirty-three thousand in 1991," according to Latin Americanist Ilene Goldman.

Judaism is also making a comeback in Cuba. Recent documentaries on the Cuban Jewish community point out that "Jews suffer along with the rest of the Cuban people." While Cuban-born Jews have maintained their religious traditions to a certain extent, they have tended to assimilate. The Jewish community has no rabbi, but during religious holy days, rabbis visit from Mexico or Canada.

Interviews in these documentaries emphasize Jewish perceptions of an absence of xenophobia and anti-semitism in Cuba. Historian Robert Levine comments that Cuba gave refuge to more Eastern European Jews during World War II than any other Latin American country.

"Even during the revolutionary government's anti-religious campaign," wrote Levine, "Castro bent over backwards not to persecute Jews." He points out that the only private enterprises not nationalized by the revolution were Jewish butchers, in order to allow Jews to keep kosher.

"Hava Nagila: the Jews in Cuba," a documentary, points out that the minority of Jews who decided to remain in Cuba after 1959 were committed to the revolution's social values.

Most Cubans who spoke with this author were not believers in any organized religion but, as one man put it, "that doesn't mean we don't believe in God. But we believe that religion is a personal thing. When it gets organized, abuses occur."

By far, my greatest cultural revelation in the realm of religion was to witness how many white Cubans were followers of Cuba's African religions, especially Santería.

Chano, the conga player who introduced Dizzy Gillespie to the layered African rhythms of Cuban music, was a follower of Abakuá, a secret African religious society with its own jargon that still exists today in Havana. Abakuá is also a form of rumba performed by the group Los Muñequitos de Matanzas.

Sitting in my friend William's living room in Old Havana, surrounded by statuettes and dolls of Santería gods and goddesses, each with little offerings before them, is for me a lasting image of the pervasive existence of Africa in Cuba.

In the Who's Who of Santería figures, the Cuban patron saint is *Nuestra Señora de Caridad* (Our Lady of Charity), a mulatto virgin. Many Cuban women are named Caridad.

There is *Oggún*, the war god, who prefers dogs as a favorite offering. I often wonder if *Oggún* has something to do with the fact that Havana is one of the few Latin American capitals without a large community of stray dogs.

Among the many other *orishas* are: *Yemanyá*, goddess of the seas, dressed in blue, who during colonial times wore the outer dress of the Blessed Virgin Mary, often referred to in the lyrics of rumba music; *Changó*, god of fire, wearing red and controlling lightning from the top of palm trees; *Obatalá*, dressed in white and associated with Christ.

"Babalawos," according to Kurlansky, "are trained to always ask questions that can be answered with no or yes—a zero or a one;" "a logical mathematical system," said one *babalawo*, which looks a lot like our binary computer systems.

In stores called *botánicas* in Cuban communities outside of Cuba, statuettes, candles, and herbs needed to practice Santería are sold.

Religious beliefs are indeed making a comeback in Cuba. But after having traveled extensively through twelve different Latin American countries, nowhere have I seen a more secular society than in Cuba. From the earlier section on Festivals, it is apparent that fewer Cuban special events are derived from religious dates than in any other Latin American country.

SENSE OF HUMOR

The Cuban sense of humor has many language-based nuances that might not be immediately understood by foreigners, and much of it is improvised according to the human relationships at hand. The most successful verbal caricatures tend to favor understatement rather than overstatement. But the more satire-oriented Cuban humor, which pokes fun of social realities, is easily understood.

In the interest of critical balance, here are two jokes of opposing viewpoints.

Q. What's the definition of socialism?
A. Socialism is the economic system between capitalism and capitalism.

An American undercover agent returns from Cuba to report on his findings. "There's no gasoline in Cuba, but the cars keep running," he babbles. "There's no food on the grocery shelves, but everybody cooks dinner. The Cubans have no money, they have nothing. Yet every night they drink rum and go dancing. I just don't get it. I just don't get it."

Cuban films from *Lucía* in the sixties to *Guantanamera* in the nineties delight in extracting humor from the most dismal and tragic events. The caricatures of Aristide in *Granma Internacional* (available at Cuban consulates or on the Internet) are examples of a sophisticated form of slapstick. (Uncle Sam, dressed as The Blockade, swings a bat against Cuba but ends up knocking down American capitalists who want to invest in the island.) Cartoons that poke fun at Cuban reality and life in general in a non-political way are found on the back page of the magazine *Bohemia*.

The Museo del Humor (Museum of Humor) is located in San Antonio de los Baños outside of Havana, and offers a panoramic history of Cuban graphic humor from 1848 to the present.

SOCIAL STATUS

Rosa Elena is a Bolivian woman, recently returned to her country after studying for nine years in Cuba, where she received a university degree, *licenciatura* (equivalent to a bachelor's degree), in chemistry. The theme of her thesis was zeolites as natural fertilizers. She had also lived and studied in Bolivia and Argentina. She makes comparisons between social status in Cuba and other Latin American societies.

"In Cuba there is no barrier between professor and student, and teachers are more demonstrative." "There is often a type of partnership between students and teachers," she added, "and teachers have

145

such a degree of self-confidence so as to be very disciplined and yet not be afraid to treat students as friends, whereas in Bolivia they maintain a greater professional distance.

"It's the same way in the society in general. In Cuba you don't feel you need to maintain appearances for social reasons. I can honestly say that I feel freer in Cuba than in any other country, and I've also spent time in Germany and Sweden besides the other countries in Latin America.

"What freedom is there in countries where you are obligated to maintain appearances based on social pretensions? For me, it's the freedom here to not have to show off this or that, to not be obligated to do things that will allow me to feel superior to others. There are some social differences in Cuba," she admitted, "but they are more cultural than based on class.

"It's not only that a person doesn't have to show off material possessions. In Bolivia, a person with a university degree must be called *Licenciado*: professionals, even the mediocre ones, fall in love with their degree, and use it to feel superior to others. This does not happen in Cuba."

"But couldn't this be a regional rather than a cultural thing?" I ask Rosa Elena. "You've referred to the Caribbean way of life and you've implied that people are less formal in tropical climates. So maybe this lack of social pretensions is simply a question of the climate. What about Santa Cruz, in your native Bolivia? It's tropical, and in that way similar to Cuba."

"In Santa Cruz, you still have people trying to feel better than others, showing off their new car, and things like that. In Cuba, even where cultural background is advantageous, professionals are considered at the same level as everyone else. It's this freedom from a system of social pretensions that I like about Cuba. For this reason, if you gave me the choice of Cuba or any other country, I'd choose Cuba."

At a social level, my own experiences generally corroborate what Rosa Elena notes about the lack of pretensions in the way Cubans address and relate to each other. In other Latin American countries, streets and buildings may be named after living people but in Cuba, even Fidel will have to die before there is ever a Castro Street. I also noticed that Cubans do not brag about their personal accomplishments. Amelia did not say she was a great cook; she said "you're going to enjoy what I prepare for you." Giselle was hardly interested that I'd written an article in a foreign newspaper about a performance of hers. Soledad seemed intrigued about doing some research for me, but saw no purpose in having her name in print.

On the other hand, there seems to exist a type of ideological pretension among bureaucrats. A European diplomat, whose name I cannot mention because of his diplomatic status, confirmed the existence of ideological pretentions within government circles.

"Cubans have much human warmth and are quite communicative," the young man said. "But I must confess that my greatest cultural barrier here has been my failure to get through the official discourse. There's a prevailing rhetoric that prevents me from communicating at a more profound level with government officials."

STATISTICS

In the film *Guantanamera*, the Cuban funeral bureaucrat is so bent on achieving successful efficiency statistics to corroborate his professional success that he grudgingly puts human concerns aside, losing his wife in the process. Like all caricatures, this one is an exaggeration of the truth. But Cuban officials do indeed want and expect to have their performance measured. My having heard a crew of diplomats cheering after the announcement that the infant mortality rate had dropped below 10 per 1,000, is anecdotal corroboration of the more flattering side of the stereotype.

VULNERABILITY

Social barriers seem to be minimal in Cuba. But what about personal barriers? If people open up and expose their vulnerability, will they

147

be embraced or taken advantage of? After many years of living in Cuba, U.S. political exile and former Black Panther member Assata Shakur told *Essence Magazine* about her surprising self-discovery in Cuba:

"Becoming aware of my own vulnerability and sensitivity and being able to express those feelings has been a surprise. In the States, I always had to be tough and ready to take care of business. Here, I can look at sides of me that are more delicate and fragile. That was kind of a shock to me ... I am a serious woman, and I want to be taken seriously, but here I don't have to live up to that Superwoman myth. I can cry and be human and lean on people who take care of me. That can be very liberating."

— Chapter Six —

THE CUBAN DRAMA

A COLLAGE OF OPINIONS

Anyone who has been in Cuba during the 1990s cannot help feeling profoundly moved by the dramatic and gripping story of a people struggling for survival. Depending on whom you talk to, the Cuban people were besieged by Uncle Sam, their own leaders, or both.

According to researchers Peter Rosset and Medea Benjamin, until its sudden and total 1991 departure, the Soviet bloc accounted for 85 percent of Cuba's trade. In the wake of a catastrophic collapse of the Cuban economy, the United States Congress enacted measures to tighten the U.S. trade embargo.

In times of extreme crisis, it is only natural for protagonists and observers alike to identify the good guys and the bad guys. In times of relative stability, it is easy for writers to remain as neutral observers. But amidst a life-and-death struggle of epic proportions, journalists traveling to Cuba have found it incredibly difficult to not take sides.

I am reminded of an old Depression song from the United States, "Which side are you on?" Acquaintances in the United States, both from the Cuban exile community and the State Department, have insinuated that my simply having been in Cuba was an act of treachery. At the same time, I know of at least one bureaucrat in the Cuban government who took measures to prevent me from writing this book, anticipating, I can only imagine, that it might in some way hurt Cuba's chances for survival.

Perhaps the ideal format for transcending the "which-side-are-you-on?" dichotomy, is a collage of contrary opinions, relating to both Cuba's crisis and and her inevitable but undefined transition. The section for Further Reading at the end of this book continues this procedure. In this chapter everyone will find both what they want to hear and what they do not want to hear. Let the sources speak for themselves.

THE EMBARGO

Even semantics can represent a journalistic "slant." How does one choose between the word "embargo" (used by the United States government) and "blockade" (used by Cuban authorities)?

No matter what one's opinion, it is apparent that the U.S. trade embargo, in it's fourth decade at this writing, will be considered a major theme in the history of Cuba in the second half of the twentieth century.

There are subtle variations of opinion on the embargo/blockade, first summarized below, and then expounded upon with specific quotes.

- the blockade is the primary cause of economic problems in Cuba;

- the embargo is totally ineffective, and Cuba's economic predicament was internally generated;

- the blockade is welcomed by Fidel Castro, and he props it up as a bogeyman, appealing to Cuban national pride, for his own political survival;

- the embargo has distorted Cuba's economy, having forced the country into dependency on Soviet-bloc goods and technology and thereby exacerbating the crisis when the Soviets pulled out;

- since no similar embargo has been enacted against other more oppressive governments (for example, the Peoples' Republic of China was granted "most-favored nation" status by the U.S. government), the "embargo" against Cuba must be construed as a symbolic statement by the United States government, warning other Latin American countries that they must fit within the U.S. economic and social paradigm;

- U.S. officials know that the embargo is ineffective, and even prefer it that way, since its main function is to secure votes from the Cuban exile community;

- the blockade excludes Cuban products from the largest consumer nation in the world (the U.S. is Cuba's most natural trading partner, based on geographical and cultural affinities). It also prevents Cuba from receiving vital spare parts, food products, and pharmaceuticals that are exclusively manufactured by United States companies or their subsidiaries abroad;

- whatever Cuba cannot sell to the United States, it makes up for by selling to Canada, Mexico, and the European community. So many countries have shown solidarity with Cuba, some in order to spite Uncle Sam, that Cuba should have been able to obtain everything it needs were its economy run efficiently;

- the embargo ironically helps Cuba's health and well-being by forcing her to use ecologically beneficial means of transportation and agriculture.

A Compendium of Views

Now we hear some of the sources for such varied points of view:

> Most of America's closest allies joined Cuba today in voting for a resolution asking Washington to end its economic embargo against Cuba.
>
> The vote in the General Assembly was 143 in favor and 3 against ...
>
> It was the sixth consecutive year that the General Assembly has called on Washington to end the embargo.
>
> Many ... nations are angry at Washington over the Helms-Burton Act, which punishes foreign companies that invest in property taken from the Americans after the 1959 revolution in Cuba.
>
> European nations say the law violates World Trade Organization rules governing trade and infringes on their sovereignty.
>
> —from "U.N. Vote Urges U.S. To End Cuban Embargo," November 5, Associated Press, as reported in the *New York Times*.

> Jorge Pérez, of Cuba's Tropical Medicine Institute, told a conference on AIDS that the American 'blockade' had ironically been a factor in helping contain the disease because of the isolation it had provided Cuba from the United States.
>
> —from "U.S. embargo kept HIV cases low, says Cuba health official," *AIDS Weekly Plus*, September 1, 1997, p. 21.

Canadian soprano sax/flute player Jane Bunnett and her husband Larry Cramer had been organizing musical exchanges with Cuban jazz musicians:

> When I first went there [to Cuba], it really hit me that there was an urgency and complexity to the music that was missing from jazz in the era of the corporate young lions ...
>
> We were well acquainted with the shortages of consumer goods brought on by the U.S. trade embargo, but we'd never seen the effect

on the schools before ... I was struck by the atrocious condition of
their instruments. One of the flutes had layers of plastic replacing the
leather pads. I couldn't get a note out of it, yet the student had been
playing Bach, Beethoven, and Debussy on it.

The Helms-Burton law that imposes penalties on foreigners who do
business with Cuba "created an immediate chill with American
music presenters and record companies because they didn't know
what it meant," said Bunnett. Concerts and club dates she had booked
for her band of Cuban musicians suddenly fell through, and negotiations for a recording deal with Sony ended abruptly.

> —from "Havana Jane," by James Hale, *Downbeat*, Nov
> 1997, p. 12.

One piece of evidence that advocates of the embargo must confront
is Castro's own actions just before Congress voted on the Helms-
Burton act. Here was a law that President Clinton had opposed and
that, therefore, faced an uphill battle. Yet on February 24, 1996, just
days before the vote, Castro had his air force shoot down two
unarmed civilian airplanes piloted by members of the Miami-based
exile group Brothers to the Rescue. No one on either side of the debate
claimed that Castro is stupid. With his awesome intelligence machine, Castro certainly knew this action would make passage of the
Helms-Burton law more likely. He presumably wanted to use it as
new ammo in his propaganda.

> —from "Why our Cuba policy is wrong," by David
> Henderson, in *Fortune*, Oct 13, 1997, p. 48–52.

What embargo? You can see American products flowing freely in
Cuba. But they only reach people with access to dollars.

> —from a recent Cuban exile interviewed for this book.

The Cuban Democracy Act of 1992 (CDA) prohibits foreign subsidiaries of U.S. corporations from selling to Cuba, thus further limiting
Cuba's access to medicine and equipment, and raising prices. In
addition, the CDA forbids ships that dock in Cuban ports from
docking in U.S. ports for six months. This drastically restricts
shipping, and increases shipping costs by some 30% ... Some
medicines and medical supplies are only available from the United

States or from foreign subsidiaries of U.S. corporations ... For example: Cuba cannot purchase spare parts for U.S. built X-ray machines ... A spare part used in the manufacture of prenatal vitamin supplements is only legally available from U.S. or subsidiary suppliers ... the Kodak X-ray film recommended by the World Health Organization for use in breast cancer screening is not available to Cuba because it is manufactured in the U.S.

U.S. owned companies increasingly dominate the world market in medicines and medical equipment, and this increasingly restricts Cuba's access to medicines and medical equipment.

—from Oxfam America and Washington Office on Latin America, "Myths and Facts about the U.S. Embargo on Medicine and Medical Supplies," 1997.

... thanks to the waivers, no European company has yet been significantly penalized under the Helms-Burton act (though it remains true that a couple of dozen of executives and their dependents are barred from entering the United States).

—from "Phoney War," *The Economist*, Oct 18, 1997.

We know how many mixed European–Cuban enterprises there are, but we don't know how many other European entrepreneurs renounced potential joint enterprises in Cuba for fear of repercussions from Helms-Burton.

Without being allowed to engage in commerce with her nearest and most natural trading partner, Cuba is obligated to take on enormous transport costs in trading with far-off countries.

Even so, so much in Cuban technological reality, for example the 110-volt system, originated from North American norms, and other countries with different technologies cannot always provide adequate substitutes.

Although I do not believe the embargo has had the effect of an all-out economic war, it is clear that it has its damaging effects. This is obvious if one considers the large numbers of potential United States tourists for whom Cuba is closed off.

—comments of a high-ranking diplomat from a European country, stationed in Cuba, and interviewed for this book.

Caught in the no-win position of violating American law or violating Canadian law, Wal-Mart Stores' Canadian unit said today that it had decided to resume sales of pajamas made in Cuba, in direct defiance of American laws ... Within hours, however, the Arkansas-based retailer said that its Canadian subsidiary had deliberately defied instructions from headquarters.

> —in summary, from "Wal-Mart Canada is Putting Cuban Pajamas Back on the Shelf," by David Sanger, *New York Times*, March 14, 1997, D4:1.

The best-known Cuban-American singer in the United States, Gloria Estefan, protested the prohibition against Cuban musicians from the island of Cuba at the September 1997 Latin American and Caribbean music fair in Miami, stemming from a Dade County law. "I cannot imagine how we could explain to the people of Cuba, who have suffered so much oppression, that the very freedoms that they so desperately desire and deserve are being annihilated in their name.

> —from "A Pinch of Salsa," *The Economist*, Oct 4, 1997.

Why do we blockade Cuba, yet grant favored-nation trading status to China? Every American president has tried to put an end to the Cuban experiment. It can't be in the name of democracy ... If that were so, we would have invaded Chile to save Chileans from Pinochet, but instead we helped put him in power ... I can only think that the United States has enforced the trade embargo for so long out of a fear that other countries might follow Cuba's attempt to keep their human and natural resources for their own use.

> —from *Cuba*, by Aaron Kufelt, p.19.

And because U.S. companies are banned from nearly all economic activities in Cuba, investors from Mexico, Italy, Spain, and Canada are scurrying to establish a business beachhead before Washington changes its mind.

> —from "It takes liberation of the imagination: foreign companies in Cuba must be creative to make a profit," by John Otis, *Houston Chronicle*, Oct 30, 1997, C1:2.

Sphere of Influence

Quotes can only go so far. Underlying reasons for foreign policy are often unstated. The U.S. presents a moral rationale for the embargo before the United Nations: "Cuba is an undemocratic society" and "the Castro government imprisons dissenters." But these arguments fail to persuade the staunchest allies of the United States because they know that the U.S. actively supported military coups against democratically elected governments in Guatemala (1953) and Chile (1973), and throughout the 1980s, backed Latin American dictators whose scale of repression (death squads, disappearances, torture) made Cuba look like a humanitarian paradise.

Since the early 1960s, the U.S. trade embargo against Cuba was based on sphere of influence. The Soviets had encroached on territory mapped out in the Monroe Doctrine. The Russians, a miliary threat, were entrenched on an island only 144 kilometers (90 miles) from Miami. If you were brought up on nightmares of a Russian nuclear attack, then you could see a logic in trying to make the Cuban people suffer just enough so that they would overthrow Fidel, and rid the U.S. of the Russian menace.

Some minority voices in the U.S. suggested that to not trade with Cuba would make Castro even more dependent on the Soviets.

When the Soviet Union self-destructed in 1991, and Russia totally abandoned Cuba, those who had reluctantly supported the embargo because of the Soviet threat now expected it to be lifted. Instead, it was enforced with a heavier hand.

My understanding of why the embargo continued during the 1990s results from my journalistic experience in various Latin American countries, and the concept of "sphere of influence."

"Yes, our votes in Senate often result from U.S. embassy pressure," former Bolivian senator, Leopoldo López confided.

Other officials told me that their nations' economic and social policies were "driven by orthodox, free-market capitalism ... because we are under the U.S. sphere of influence."

If one believes that unbridled capitalism is the answer to poverty and social ills in Latin America, then one should be able to see a political reason for supporting the embargo. Cuba may still represent a socialist alternative to free-market neo-liberalism; if that alternative were allowed to spread to neighboring countries, the U.S. plutocracy would no longer be the master of its own sphere of influence.

Some Cuban-Americans close to the embargo issue will disagree with my "realpolitik" appraisal. "The [embargo] policy," wrote Cuban-American journalist Richard Estrada, "is being driven largely by special interest pleading by Cuban-American conservatives based in Miami."

Such lobbying does exist, of course, but, are Cuban-American conservatives using the U.S. government, or are orthodox, free-market ideologues with the government using the Cuban-Americans?

A significant number of Cuban-Americans, most of whom oppose Castro, have already voted against the embargo in a visceral way, by sending money to relatives and friends in Cuba.

Whatever the real political reasons for continuing the embargo (stopping the spread of socialism within the U.S. sphere of influence, or gaining votes from Cuban-Americans), such reasons are left officially unpronounced, displaced in international forums by totally ineffective moralistic rationale.

U.S. Businesses

The United States Department of Commerce has been granting permission for United States corporations to explore business possibilities in Cuba, in anticipation of the inevitable end to the trade embargo and related congressional acts against business with Cuba. A large sector of the United States business community, accustomed to an advantage in the international arena of commerce, feels frustrated that Europeans, Canadians, Mexicans, and Asians have been ceded the upper hand by its own government.

Those American business representatives eager to establish a beachhead in Cuba were particularly elated when the Pope condemned the U.S. trade embargo as inhumane during his January 1998 visit to Cuba.

DON'T WORRY, BE HAPPY: MUSIC IN CUBA

The embargo may have an impact on the number of obtainable new musical instruments and on spare parts for old ones, but it has had little impact on an exciting Cuban music scene. In fact, Cuban salsa ranks second to U.S. pop music in international export success. There are more than thirty Japanese salsa bands, for example, and Cuban CDs flow freely around the world, even within the United States.

Although Cuban jazz does not have a great internal market, music from groups like Irakere or individuals like Gonzalo Rubalcaba are on the cutting edge of contemporary jazz. From Paris to Manhattan,

many jazz groups are obligated to study Cuban rhythms just to keep apace.

In many books on Cuba, the music receives a few paragraphs as one of the facets of culture. But Cuban culture *is* music, and music is and will continue to be one of the great adventures in contemporary Cuba.

Serge Kasimoff, a former student of mine, is an American keyboard player who began his career as a prodigy in both classical and jazz music. He presents one very visceral model for how to adopt a new culture. The sensorial medium for his total adjustment to Cuban culture was the music and dance. When he signed up for my Spanish class in the early eighties, he was only beginning to explore Cuban history and culture. I remember him telling me that he was bent on getting a feel for the Cuban way of life by dancing and jamming with Cuban musicians until he'd absorbed it all.

"I started hearing Cuban rhythms around the age of twelve, when I was listening to a jazz station that had a Monday night Latin jazz program."

He'd listen to Santana's "Abraxas," Herbie Mann's "Memphis Underground," and Cal Tjader's "Live at the Funky Quarters," "but I didn't know at the time that these were Cuban rhythms."

When he was in his early twenties, the jazz brass players he was working with invited him to Cuban jam sessions. The legendary Cal Tjader triggered his total immersion into Cuban music.

When I visited Serge's Hollywood apartment at the beginning of 1998, I learned that he had traveled three times to Cuba on music study visits, and that he was playing regularly with two Afro-Cuban music groups in Los Angeles.

We discussed the history of Cuban rhythms and harmonies and analyzed just how and why Cuban music has become so vital throughout the world. As we talked, Serge banged out different riffs on the piano to add reality to his words.

Serge's earliest salsa gigs were at California Cuban social clubs in 1981. He then decided that it would be necessary to know all the other musical parts and not just the piano.

"Eventually I was drawn more and more to Cuban music," he says, "its jazziness, earthiness.

"The first Cuban group I heard in person was at the carnival in Vera Cruz, Mexico, in 1986. It was called Orquesta Ritmo Tropical. It was one of my great life experiences, not only because of the unusual syncopations but because of the unexpected exchange I had with the musicians. I was surprised how they'd offered me, a stranger: *would you like to copy our music?*"

Serge was impressed by their willingness to share their creativity, "because they're so secure in what they know," he says. At that moment, he knew that he would eventually have to go to Cuba to see, hear, and participate in what was happening.

Guantanamera

If one were tracing the heritage of contemporary Cuban music, it would be necessary to go back to several intrinsic music genres. The *punto guajiro* is Cuban country music. The most famous song from this genre, *La Guantanamera*, was composed in 1929 by Joseíto Fernández. It began as a simple stanza to which improvised *décimas* were conjured up by dueling guitarists, in an ancient oral tradition of call-and-response. Beginning in 1948 and lasting for twelve years, Fernández used the song as background for singing a tabloid version of the news. The program was immensely popular, and led to a black-and-white documentary about *El Punto Cubano*, filmed in the early years of the Revolution.

As a gesture of solidarity to the Cuban Revolution, U.S. folk singer Pete Seeger performed the song, now to the words of a José Martí poem, at a 1963 Carnegie Hall concert in New York, and the song became an international hit.

The extraordinary evolution of *La Guantanamera* continues today with the 1997 hit movie by the same name, with the lyrics of the song serving as a chorus for a dark comedy about the Special Period. This last film by the late Cuban film maker Tomás Gutiérrez Alea, grossed over US $800,000. Such a complex evolution of such a simple tune has made *La Guantanamera* an international cultural icon.

Curiously, José Martí's simple lyrics are a reminder that Cuba is not simply a country of sea coasts:

> my verse is a wounded deer
> who seeks refuge in the mountains ...
> With the poor people of the earth
> I want to throw my luck
> With the poor people of the earth
> I want to throw my luck
> the stream in the mountains
> fulfills me more than the sea.

The Son *and Other Genres*

Guajira mountain music was one of many genres of Cuban music. *Charanga* music was played by an *orquesta típica* for a dancing

161

public, and the *danzón,* with more Spanish influence, as the dance of the people. The *bolero* is a more hybrid romantic music with guitar accompaniment, not exclusively a Cuban form, but popular among today's roving musicians.

But the most powerful influence in contemporary Cuban music has been the *son*, a musical form that maintains a life of its own and has enjoyed a contemporary resurgence. Papi Oviedo y sus Soneros and Sierra Maestra are two of many groups producing recordings at this time. A compilation of various *son* groups is found on an album called *Casa de la Trova*.

The *son* divides into two sub-genres, one rural, from El Oriente, and the other urban, called *rumba*, centering in Matanzas.

Papi Oviedo plays the *tres*, a guitar of three double strings, and one of the six original instruments within this genre. The *clave* is comprised of two wooden sticks tapped together in syncopation, the most piercing of several layered rhythms. The *bongó* is a pair of small drums whose fuller sound contrasts with the *clave*. A thumb piano with five metal keys in a wooden box, of West African origin, is called the *marímbola*. Add a guitar and maracas, and you have the original *son* sextet.

The sextet became a septet in the 1920s when a trumpet was added, a combination initiated by the Septeto Habanero. The source of today's salsa may come from Arsenio Rodríguez, who added two more trumpets to the septet, as well as taller drums called *congas* in 1946.

"Much early salsa was putting new clothes on old music," says Serge, my musician friend. Today, many leaders of salsa bands are *conga* players.

Along with the *son* came other great Cuban genres of less impact in today's scene, including the *cha cha cha*, which some say was invented for those with less dexterity, and the *mambo*, whose most famous band leader was Pérez Prado.

Many contemporary musicians are well-versed in all of these genres, so one often hears cross-over sounds. The most famous salsa group, Los Van Van, who have accumulated the most international frequent traveler miles, have *charanga* influence in their spirited salsa and a warm and contagious sound, whose joy is a great antidote for the Special Period.

The contemporary *rumba*, an urban, folk, street music and much more complex than the popularized rumbas of the 1950s, is an experience in itself. No one can listen to Los Muñequitos de Matanzas, especially their album *Rumba Caliente,* without wanting to take the next flight to Cuba. The most popular form of the rumba is called *guaguancó.* The singer recounts an everyday event, to be challenged by the chorus. Then, the rumba breaks out (*se rompe la rumba*) and the pair of dancers dance the *vacunao* (meaning: vaccinated or pricked). With movements of sexual possession, the man moves his waist, one hand or a leg towards the woman, who tries to elude him.

Original instruments for the rumba were makeshift wood boxes with different pitches when struck, with sharper percussive sounds coming from pairs of spoons or a spoon against a glass bottle. Original rumbas were accompanied exclusively by percussive instruments, with the chorus functioning as an orchestra. Today these sounds are reproduced with more formal and varied instrumentation.

Rumba is more than a form of music. It is a neighborhood festivity, reminiscent in spirit with the blues "juke joint" in the Mississippi Delta, or the more religious *candomblé* in northeastern Brazil. Although rumba originates in the West African Yoruba culture, white Spanish descendents at the bottom of the Cuban social scale were totally integrated within the rumba culture.

Rumba groups like Los Muñequitos de Matanzas, Afrocuba de Matanzas, and Cutumba from Santiago are known as *portadores* (carriers), since they have inherited the artistic and expressive traditions of the original rumba and are direct descendents of the *coros de rumba*, neighborhood groups from the previous century. What is known today as salsa music borrows heavily from rumba tradition.

Cuba's isolation during the embargo and the country's Africani-zation because of white flight has led to new and exciting develop-ments in salsa. The rhythms have grown so complex that fabled New York salsa sounds simple in comparison. Each Cuban group has wanted to not sound like the guy next door, and there is no homogeniz-ing marketing mechanism to conform to a niche audience as there would be in other more commercial countries, so virtually every musical experience in Cuba will offer a surprise.

Salsa musicians know their rhythm and blues and some have blended that genre into what Serge calls a "cross-cultural feast."

"The surrealness of living in Cuba in the uncertain nineties, with a little bit of anarchy," according to Serge, has led to what he calls "*La música del período especial.*"

"Because of the embargo, some Cuban music was able to develop in its own Petri dish, without having to compete in free market systems."

In Cuba the next great musical surprise is right around the corner.

Along with the various forms of salsa, a separate genre of sung poetry called *La Nueva Trova* and more straight-ahead jazz are both extremely popular internationally although they sustain a smaller, more exclusive audience within Cuba. The haunting *Nueva Trova* melodies and poetry of both Pablo Milanés and Silvio Rodríguez have become part of the repertoire of folk and protest singers around the world. The jazz piano of Gonzalo Rubalcaba, and groups like Irakere are the "Jazz Messengers" of contemporary international jazz.

Other contemporary groups no less astonishing include Jesús Alemany's Cubanismo, the Afro-rumba group Bamboleo, Latin jazz artist Issac Delgado, La Charanga Habanera, Los Muñequitos de Matanzas, NG La Banda, and The Afro-Cuban All-Stars. Serge's group Máquina Loca allows U.S. citizens isolated from Cuba during the embargo to experience this musical tradition in a live setting.

Like Serge, many of the best salsa musicians have formal training in classical music. NG La Banda's José Luis Cortés, nicknamed "El Tosco," studied under the great Cuban classical composer Harold Gramatges. In 1997, at the age of 79, Gramatges was awarded the prestigious Tomás Luis de Victoria prize in Madrid for his symphonic creations. Gramatges recognizes that "there can be superb creations in pop music as well as some terrible pieces in classical music." He, like Giselle Grau's teacher Andrés Alén, harbors no genre prejudices. Cuba's music teachers only demand high quality for a demanding public.

"Nobody can get by on just hype," says Serge. "You gotta play … even the taxi driver knows who's good, who can play. This is one of the most musical cultures in the world."

In fact, on any street in any Cuban city or town you will hear accomplished but virtually anonymous musicians, known by nick-names by the people in their cities. Serge had fulfilled his dream and traveled three times to Cuba to soak in the *ambiente*, but he hasn't had enough.

"The first breath after arriving at José Martí Airport in Havana," says Serge, "is a sweetness like nowhere else in the Caribbean. Maybe it's all the sugar cane in the air."

"These people move their hips too well," I once said to Soledad, as we listened to a salsa band in Old Havana. "I'm too embarrassed to get up with these flashy dancers."

"That's okay," she said. "The important thing is to love the music."

The love of music should have calmed the savage breast, but Cuban musicians from the United States who have traveled to Cuba have risked being blackballed from clubs when they return. When Los Van Van arrived in Miami, they were greeted with a protest at the airport by white Cubans. Black Cubans from Miami, even though they were anti-Fidel, supported Los Van Van.

In 1997, jazzman Gonzalo Rubalcaba went to perform in Miami's Gusman Center for the Performing Arts. He was met by "a mob of 500 angry, shouting, flag-waving, and flag-throwing anti-Castro demonstrators."

The apolitical Rubalcaba does not even live in Cuba. (He resides in Santo Domingo). But he earned the hostile reception for not having renounced the Cuban system that had given him his free training. He began formal piano studies at the age of nine and earned a degree in music composition from Havana's Institute of Fine Arts. As a teenage prodigy, he performed with bebop trumpeter Dizzy Gillespie, who became one of the Cuban pianist's greatest fans. With his classical training and interest in many types of music, Rubalcaba's jazz remains eclectic and without commercial trappings.

Contemporary Cuban music seems to lack a market niche. "Unlike the blues," says American guitarist Ry Cooder, "the music has not been destroyed by commercialization. There's no music business in that Tin Pan Alley way. Musicians cannot accumulate vast wealth, and they have never been put on a pedestal. That is why the music is so heartfelt. In a way, it just isn't part of the modern world."

Cooder traveled to Cuba to record veteran Cuban *son, guajira,* and *danzón* musicians, most of them in their seventies and eighties, in a milestone CD called *Buena Vista Social Club.*

"I'm not worried about the politics," Cooder said. "It's not even an issue. But you've got to stand up for what's right sometimes, and so I suppose it is a little bit of a statement."

Serge's visits to Cuba had nothing to do with politics and everything to do with music.

"Cuban music will survive in spite of the politics," says Serge. "Politicians will come, live and die, but the music will remain. Cuban culture is much more potent than the politics."

TRANSITIONS

Someone should write a novel about Cuba like Marge Piercy's *Woman on the Edge of Time,* which alternates between two possible

futures, one of utopian socialism and the other of unbridled capitalism. But a Cuban novel would have to be more complex, with several
more possible futures. In fact, the two extremes of the political
probability spectrum are the most unlikely of Cuba's futures. Utopian
socialism is not apt to escalate in the shadow of a massive and
inherently capitalistic tourism industry. On the other hand, the primitive capitalism that characterized Cuba before 1959 and Russia after
the fall of communism will not be tolerated by even the most diehard
anti-Castro Cubans on the island.

"We want change," said Arnulfo, a former communist militant
now disenchanted with the social divisions of the dual economy. "But
we don't want change imposed from abroad. Cubans should be
allowed to decide their own destiny."

Just about everyone agrees that Cuba is changing, passing through
a transition. But transition implies moving from one phase to the next,
and no one has defined what the next phase will be. Some of the
measures of the Special Period seem to be leading toward a mixed
economy, part free-market, part socialized, but other measures may
have been intended as a temporary and expedient means to defend
socialism. A silent tug-of-war is taking place, between the global
economy on one end, and the Cuban people on the other.

There are certain things that the public has learned to take for
granted. "Cubans cannot conceive of a market system for their health
care," said economist Pablo Ramos, chancellor of Bolivia's national
university in La Paz and observer of the Cuban scene.

"Cubans can accept small fees for sports and cultural activities,"
explained Dr. Jorge Crisosto, originally from Chile. Crisosto does
volunteer work in Cuba, and admires the health system to such an
extent that he chose Cuba over other countries to send his mother for
complicated surgery. "But the people will not accept the exorbitant
ticket fees of other countries."

Barring military invasion, everything seems to point toward a
mixed economy with both capitalist and socialist components, with

inalienable rights retained and nurtured for education, culture, and health care.

Success can sometimes bring problems. "In Cuba," continues Dr. Crisosto, "medical care is prioritized without distinction for ability to pay or geographic region. They've even created a mechanical heart that can be used by a patient while awaiting a heart transplant. Such advances are unheard of in other poor countries.

"But these successes create problems. As life expectancy increases, so do geriatric needs, and the cost of the system escalates.

"In other Latin American countries, people wait too late to seek care for financial reasons. In Cuba, we have the opposite problem, as Cubans often go to a doctor too early, before it is necessary. People are going to have to become accustomed to paying moderate fees."

When forecasting what will happen to Cuba in the upcoming years, many analysts label the eventual turning point as the death of Fidel Castro. They have assumed that each and every public policy decision in Cuba in the 1990s was ordered or coerced by Fidel. They fail to take into account that Cuba's education system has produced an abundant pool of professionals and technicians, to the extent that Cuba exports its expertise to other countries.

Some of these products of the education system retain a utopian perspective and undertake quixotic experiments, not because they have been commanded to do so but out of a fervent belief in their mission. Economists, for example, continue to attempt creative and never-before-tried adjustments of capitalist enterprise in order to retain a social component and prevent the type of third world–first world internal clashes that plague other Latin American countries. Some measures seem to have a modicum of success, while others fail and are quickly abandoned.

With no precedents from other countries, a trial-and-error mode prevails as the only means to retain the advances of social equality while administering controlled infusions of capitalism.

Organic Agriculture

One extraordinary idealistic experiment worthy of marquee billing is the effort by Cuban agronomists to consummate a massive transformation to organic agriculture. It was a risky proposition to choose the height of the Special Period for such an unprecedented change in the whole culture of food production. Other countries have proceeded with a great deal more caution, with incremental increases in organic farming.

Cuba was betting on its human resources. With only 2 percent of the population of Latin America but 11 percent of its scientists, the government hoped that human wisdom could compensate for the cutoff of pesticides, herbicides, and vital parts needed for more mechanized farming. "Biofertilizers and biopesticides, microbial formulations that are non-toxic to humans," were used to replace the chemical varieties, even though "empirical evidence ... demonstrates that it can take anywhere from three to five years to achieve levels of productivity that prevailed beforehand," according to Dr. Peter Rosset and Medea Benjamin, researchers in agricultural ecology and authors of *The Greening of the Revolution: Cuba's Experiment with Organic Agriculture*.

In fact, to reach previous levels of productivity was not nearly enough, since food supplies from the Soviets and East Europeans that had complemented local production had been cut off. The conversion to organic agriculture was undertaken precisely at a moment in history when the Cuban population was on the verge of severe hunger and malnutrition.

Ironically, the "classical model" of agriculture employed previously in Cuba was the same that had been encouraged by *both* the United States and the Soviet Union in their spheres of influence. The model, as it applied to Cuba, includes extensive monoculture of export crops, often not native to the region, through a highly mechanized system that depends on imported technology and inputs (fertilizers, pesticides, etc.). Throughout the third world, mechanization

A cane cutter. Through 1990, Cuba's monocultural export economy, based on sugar, was a vestige of colonialism. A more diversified agriculture is now developing.

drives hordes of rural inhabitants to cities, causing unresolvable social ills. Such a massive scale of single-crop farming erodes and salinates the soil. As plants develop pesticide resistance, ever escalating amounts of chemical pesticides are needed.

In third world countries like Bolivia and Mexico I have known firsthand the tribulations of being obligated to investigate the source of my family's food. Are the tomatoes laden with pesticides? Is cow milk laced with hormones? Am I poisoning my children? Often, the answer I found was, yes.

171

Cuba's "alternative model," referred to as low-input sustainable agriculture, uses non-chemical plants and microbes, avoids dependence on heavy machinery, and diversifies and rotates crops. The experiment was initiated in the early nineties. By mid-1993, it appeared as if a food crisis was about to reach a level of desperation.

But little by little, outdoor farmers' markets began to sprout up in urban neighborhoods. Healthy produce like avocados, cucumbers, oranges, and bananas, as well as pork meat, became available with prices that fit within budgets based on Cuban salaries. Some shortages still exist, but according to Dr. Rosset, "Cuba has overcome a food shortage with little use of pesticides or fertilizers, an example to be looked at closely by other countries."

Ironically, a post-embargo Cuba may be forced to return to some aspects of the classic model of agriculture for reasons of expediency or because foreign investors offering vital currency may require it.

Rosa Elena, the Bolivian student in Cuba quoted earlier in this book, will be proud to learn that her graduate thesis on the use of ziolites as natural fertilizers has played a role in the successful conversion of a large part of Cuba's agriculture to an organic model.

Mixed or Mixed-Up Economy?

Inevitably, the global economy will have a major impact on Cuba. A dramatic episode of the transition period will be based on the precarious attempt to preserve a culture that has emphasized sharing and solidarity even as the world-wide consumer culture is allowed to co-exist. Will Cubans prefer styrofoam burger chains over their homespun *paladares*? Will economic "growth" be spread evenly enough to prevent the social problems that plague the Venezuelas, Mexicos, and El Salvadors of Latin America? Are there other models of mixed economies such as France or Denmark that could be applied in a Caribbean way?

Whatever shall happen in Cuba, these will be tremendously exciting times, Fidel or no Fidel, and the inherent culture clash between utopianism and an unbridled market economy will be manifest in various arenas of Cuban society.

New Emigration

During this transition period, new social paradigms will emerge. For example, I discovered a new type of Cuban emigrant, one that does not fit with previous prototypes. Arnulfo was a dedicated socialist, member of the Communist Party, and a foreman in a milk factory who earned US$ 7 per month. He left Cuba not because of socialism but because of what he called "the effects of neoliberal reforms."

Arnulfo was emotionally drained by the social divisions caused by the introduction of dollars in the economy, and felt that tourism was introducing a type of corruption that had not existed since 1959. With access to dollars from relatives abroad, Arnulfo was embarrassed and discouraged that he was living with privileges that other Cubans lacked.

"The blockade is 90 percent to blame," he said, "but we made our errors, too. Fidel is losing control. We hope it is not too late for him to be remembered for the good things he did."

Women

Also at stake during the transition period is the independence of Cuban women. Olga Gasaya, vice-chair of the Department of Psychology at the University of Havana has discovered, through comprehensive research, that "in spite of their high level of social and professional achievement and public status, most women still perceive their fundamental role as wife or housewife.

"But the higher achieving they were, the greater the sense of guilt at not being able to fulfill a role in the home. And others who chose to stay at home felt guilt for not participating in professional life."

Younger Cuban women who have not felt what it is like to live in more male-dominated societies of other Latin American countries, take the gains in status of women for granted, but remain fiercely independent.

Given the high level of self-esteem among Cuban women, I wondered how there could be a resurgence of prostitution.

"I haven't done formal research on prostitution," said Gasaya in a radio interview. "But I believe it's connected to the economic crisis. But this crisis affects most women to the same degree. All women look for ways to solve the crisis, but only a small percentage of them resort to prostitution. I think that within this small percentage, many suffer from problems of self-esteem, since there are other methods of self-employment with which women can make good money.

"These are *not* the type of prostitutes that exist in other Latin American countries," she added, "where it's done for survival. It's very sad and painful for this country, which has made so many strides in the advancement of women."

It is precisely for this reason that the re-emergence of prostitution in Cuba has received such widespread press coverage. No one writes feature articles about widespread prostitution in Mexico and Central America. But for better or for worse, Cuba has been held to a higher standard. If increasing economic growth can be spread evenly throughout Cuban society, the new wave of prostitution should subside once again.

The visit of the Pope in January of 1998 and his call for more traditional roles for women does not seem to have encouraged Cuban women to drop their use of birth control devices and abortion, nor to convince them to marry a man before first living with him and becoming convinced that he will be trustworthy and faithful.

Unlike other third world countries, Cuba has maintained a low birth rate, comparable to developed nations, and Cuban women's groups do not want a return to the unbridled population growth that plagues other Latin American countries.

Consumer Culture

Perhaps the greatest uncertainty during Cuba's transition relates to the worldwide consumer culture. Many people are attracted to a place like Cuba because, in the absence of McDonald's, recreational shopping, new cars, glitzy commercial districts, throwaway plastic bottles, commercial TV, and a celebrity industry, the philosophy of "the best things in life are free" has been converted into an art form.

A day at the beach, dancing, playing or watching baseball, volleyball or basketball, street festivals, and mainly hanging out with friends and neighbors, these are all major pastimes in Cuba that don't cost a penny. You don't have to go shopping to be happy. In fact, the concept of shopping relates strictly to obtaining what one needs.

Someone should invent a happiness gauge. Cubans complain a lot, but even griping seems to be a pastime. Is it possible that those Cubans who, by choice or obligation, remain without a consumer culture have been just as happy as the throngs in the shopping malls of the surrounding countries?

Could crime statistics be a gauge of happiness? Why is it that Havana, even during the desperation of the Special Period, had such a small proportion of crime compared to Mexico City, Caracas, Lima, or San Salvador? Could it be that Cuba's sense of community has replaced the need for keeping ahead of the Joneses? With the opening of the economy, will sense of commodity replace a sense of community?

Thus far, businesses entering Cuba and catering to the local population operate in a mode of fulfilling needs rather than creating needs. Many foreign entrepreneurs seem socially committed to preserving Cuba's human ecology. But that may change.

For the next decade, Cuba figures to be one of the most exciting places in the world. The last of Cuba's neocolonial patrons, the Soviets, are gone. Cuba is now an independent nation. Let's hope that geopolitics of any stripe will not interfere with the Cubans' own right to determine their destiny, whatever that may be. With the syncopated accompaniment of *salsa* rhythms, Cuba offers glorious beaches, a remarkable level of racial harmony, a profound sense of community, an exuberant spirit, and freedom from social and gender-based pretensions.

— Chapter Seven —

SURVIVAL SKILLS

Prior to my arrival in Havana, I sought advice from every traveler I could find, every guidebook, every travel agency specializing in Cuba. Never before in my travel plans had I been so painstaking in seeking guidance. And never before had I received such bad advice from such good experts.

How could such seasoned travelers, perceptive writers, and expert tour agents be the source of such useless and sometimes prejudiced advice? And how could I avoid the same pitfalls in this book?

Cuba is in a process of transformation, and from one moment to the next, what was right becomes wrong, and what was prohibited becomes encouraged. For example, religion was once the "opium of

177

the people," but Cubans were officially encouraged to get out and see the Pope during his 1998 visit.

The most important piece of advice is, upon arrival, to enjoy the inevitable conversations with Cubans and ask them whatever you need to know. In every neighborhood, there are people to guide you. If you're not confident with the response of one person, get a "second opinion" or triangulate: ask three different people the same question.

You may trust most of the information that is offered for free. But beware of the well-meaning citizen who prefers to respond on hearsay rather than admit he doesn't know.

LANGUAGE

Many Cubans speak fine English, but for most strategic communication, some Spanish is essential. It is highly recommended that the non-Spanish-speaking potential traveler to Cuba take a continuing education course in Spanish prior to departure. Students in not-for-credit continuing education courses are usually more motivated than their counterparts in required university credit courses. Continuing education courses are often more practical, with abstract theory kept at a strategic minimum.

Most Spanish grammar is similar to that of English, with a few important but easily understood exceptions, such as more extensive verb conjugations, placement of adjectives after nouns, two separate verbs "to be," etc.

Spanish is a phonetic language. Once students master the five simple vowel sounds: (a = ah; e = eh; i = shortened ee; o = oh; u = shortened oo), they are in a position to understand and use thousands of cognates (words that are identical or quite similar between the two languages).

Example: virtually every word ending in "ion" in English is similar in Spanish, such as *conversación, comunicación, intuición, nación*, etc., and most derivatives from these "ion" words will also be cognates.

Cuban Spanish has a unique nasal sing-song, with glossed-over consonants sometimes difficult to perceive. Variations in the Spanish language from one country to another, however, are far fewer than variations in English between Massachusetts, New Orleans, London, Ireland, and Australia.

Most Cubans display remarkable patience with visitors who speak broken Spanish. Spanish has both a formal and familiar way to address people. The formal "you" is *usted* and the familiar "you" is *tú* (each with its own verb conjugation). The best method for deciding whether or not to use the familiar or the formal is to listen to how you are addressed by a particular person, and then to address him or her in the same way. Most Cubans are quick to use the familiar form of address.

Important social tip: once you are addressed with the familiar *tú*, it would be an insult to respond in the formal.

Follow-up Spanish courses, once you are in Cuba, are listed in the Cuba Crib Sheet.

NEIGHBORHOOD

As has been noted, the most practical way of establishing roots in Cuba is to hang out in a neighborhood of choice. Find out who your neighborhood's "public characters" are. They could be a bartender, or a street hustler, the operator of a beauty parlor, an enterprising youngster, a hotel concierge, a street vendor.

Once these people have seen you more than once, they are more likely to offer helpful advice. This concept of staying within a neighborhood goes against the grain of even the best travel guides, which operate on the encyclopaedic assumption that the more places you visit in the shortest time, the more quickly you will adapt.

In Cuba, the fewer places in which you spend the most time will offer a newcomer the greatest chance to become part of a sense of place and culture.

CURRENCY

Consider the following example of bad advice. I had read in several travel guides that it was more practical for foreigners to use dollars and not get involved with the local currency, the Cuban peso. The problem with this advice was that nearly half of all Cubans did not use dollars. Functioning exclusively within the dollar economy would leave the newcomer segregated from a large sector of Cuban society. Furthermore, tourist establishments functioning exclusively in dollars are the scene where hustlers, those in need of dollars, would see newcomers as consumers of cigars, rum, sex, or other commodities. While many of these hustlers are interesting characters, and some quite helpful, after a while, it is a relief to go to places where you are just another human being and not the object of a sales pitch.

The simple act of changing dollars to Cuban pesos and then patronizing establishments that operate with the local currency will

With the reforms of the mid-90s, private, family-run businesses dealing in Cuban pesos have sprung up everywhere. If you want to be part of the real Cuba, change your dollars to Cuban pesos and patronize these businesses.

put the visitor in realistic Cuban scenarios, untainted by the contradictions of tourism.

I would drink my beer in two different bars in the same neighborhood. At the first bar, which dealt only in dollars, most of the Cuban patrons were there to sell something to the tourist. But at the bar that used Cuban pesos, the scene was much more authentic, and conversations were not initiated with an ultimate objective of selling something. Without trying to save money, the same beer that cost a dollar (equivalent to 23 Cuban pesos) at the dollar establishment, cost only 14 pesos at the bar dealing in local currency.

Cuba's currency situation will undoubtedly change, but in the meantime, when I asked people in the neighborhood to direct me to the most authentic places, I was usually pointed to establishments that dealt in Cuban pesos. My neighbors also told me where I could change money, both legally and under the table (if I needed change quickly and the legal change window was closed). A most convenient change booth in Havana is found on the northeast corner across from Parque Central.

TRANSPORTATION

Another piece of bad advice came from a tour agent who specialized in travel to Cuba and visited Cuba four times a year. "Take taxis," she said. "The buses are undependable and the bus system is too complicated."

I figured that I wasn't going to survive in any place for long if I had to take a taxi every time I wanted to go anywhere. I also figured that since most Cubans use buses and cannot afford taxis, I would not be living the life of most Cubans if I were to get around by taxi on a regular basis.

Regular buses are referred to as *guaguas* and the double-humped monsters pulled by truck cabins are called *camellos*. The *camellos* seem to lumber around for lengthy periods without needing a drink of scarce petroleum. When you see these beasts of human burden, they

181

are always packed, and you wonder how anyone ever gets a seat. (More seats will become available as more public vehicles can be put into service as soon as Cuba gains greater access to petroleum at fairer prices.)

In the meantime, to land a seat on any type of bus, the best strategy is to find the first stop. It is better to walk a few blocks to the first stop, wait on line and get a seat, than to remain several stops nearer your destiny and enter a packed vehicle. In Havana, a first stop of many lines is Parque de la Fraternidad, conveniently located south of Parque Central.

But what if you are nowhere near a first stop? Don't schedule activities one after another. Leave time to wait for the bus, and you can actually enjoy that time by engaging in conversations with the people who are waiting with you. Waiting is not all that bad in a country where people actually talk to each other.

An alternative to a long wait is to take a *colectivo*. This is a collective taxi that charges per person. You don't find the *colectivo*; it finds you. A bus will cost less than one Cuban peso, usually about 40 cents. A *colectivo* within the city might cost about 10 pesos, much more than the bus but considerably less than a taxi.

Private cars may also be used as taxis. These unofficial taxis cost less than regular taxis but more than *colectivos*. In the *coches particulares*, you might find that your driver is a doctor who has been given the use of a car as a perk to make up for his low salary. Usually, your all-purpose neighborhood hustler can find you a *coche particular*.

If you want none of this, consider taking apart your bicycle and packing it with you as luggage to Cuba.

I found that public transportation in Cuba, during a time of economic crisis and fuel shortage, was much better than it looked. Yes, the buses were crowded. But people waiting in line or standing within a bus were always civil in their behavior, no matter how uncomfortable the situation.

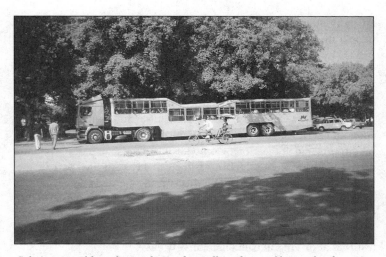

Cuba's unusual bus, the two-humped camello, *a beast of human burden going many miles without thirst for gasoline.*

Years ago, I traveled through ten countries of Latin America by hitchhiking. In Cuba, hitching is called *hacer botella* (to make a bottle). It is a common custom, especially outside the city, and drivers are encouraged by the government to pick up hitchhikers. I never hitchhike in Cuba, since Cubans with less spare time than I have need the ride a lot more than I do. If you've rented a car and are traveling in the country, remember that if the oil shortage is still limiting bus service, it is customary to pick up hitchhikers.

Cuban hitchhikers are usually villagers who need to get somewhere. They are not the adventurous backpackers you'd see in Europe or the grizzly anarchists on the road in the United States. Government officials, called *amarillos* because of their yellow uniforms, are on site to help arrange rides.

With so few cars on the road in Cuba, renting a car is a comfortable alternative, especially if you are planning on visiting parts of rural Cuba inaccessible by train or bus. In most cultures, the automobile is an individualistic tool that tends to isolate the driver from other people. In Cuba, it's the opposite. A private driver fulfills a public service by picking up citizens and gets to know people along the way.

Gas prices are at a European level, and car rental prices are set at rates that conform to a tourist's capacity to pay. Most hotels will lead you to the nearest car rental agency, which often has an office inside the hotel itself. Officially-sanctioned rent-a-car companies are the economical Havanautos (at airports and major hotels) and Cubanacan (at airports and at the Hotel Comodoro). Cubanacan has a "fly-and-drive" plan, through which a visitor can drive to any part of the country with an airport and then drop off the car and take a flight.

Most readers will not be renting cars, so an exhaustive list of Cuban driving rules is best obtained directly from the rental agency. After having driven for years in Mexico and Central America, I can testify that driving in Cuba is relatively easy.

If you've got time on your hands, and specific places are not as important to you as traveling itself, I'd recommend traveling by train. Cuba is the only country in the Caribbean with a passenger train system. At the train station, do not go by posted schedules, which have probably changed. I found the service at the Havana train station quite friendly.

The problem with train travel is that it is limited geographically. For example, a train will take you from Havana to the city of Pinar del Río, but from there, you'll have to hitch or hike to get to Pinar del Río's main attraction, tobacco-growing country in the lush green valley of Viñales.

Air travel is relatively inexpensive within Cuba and to Cuba from nearby places like Cancún. But beware. Schedules often change. I once arrived at the José Martí airport an hour before my scheduled flight only to discover that the plane was about ready to depart. They had moved the departure time ahead by an hour! I would have been there two hours in advance, but the "transfer" that was supposed to pick me up never arrived.

Buying a voucher for an airport "transfer" for a later date is not a good idea. On the other hand, the agency that had sold me the phantom transfer, Sol Y Son, graciously returned my money, and I've had nothing but good experiences otherwise with Sol Y Son.

HOUSING

Housing is scarce, and in a country that prides itself on sheltering all its citizens, apartments are simply not available to foreigners, unless they are diplomats. The easiest way for a newcomer to survive financially in the realm of housing is to live with a family. Word of mouth remains the best way to find family lodging. Seasoned travelers to Cuba arrive with a hotel voucher for three days and then let their neighbors find them a room with a family. The government is in the process of legislating a system of family lodging. If such legislation is eventually enacted, the traveler will have access to lists of approved families.

I've known other foreigners who decide to live in a hotel. (Hotels are listed in the Cuba Crib Sheet.) They are able to take their meals with a family, which is healthier and more economical than eating in restaurants on a daily basis.

TOURS

The tours one finds in hotel lobbies through the government company Havanatur are usually quite pleasant. But the best part comes if you can get the guide to depart from his or her script. The guides themselves seem to enjoy the tour even more when customers ask probing questions.

There are a number of specialty tour companies originating outside of Cuba that offer package deals that are unprecedented in the tourist industry, in that they involve participation between clients and Cubans in a particular profession. These tours may specialize in medicine, ecology, music, agriculture, architecture, or virtually any other field. I have never taken any of these tours, but I've interviewed many people who have, and have never found anyone who came away disappointed. The price is not cheap but the service is enthusiastic and intellectually honest. If travel restrictions for people from the United States have not yet been lifted by the time you see this book, such tours will facilitate your getting permission from the United States Department of Commerce.

The names and contact numbers of some of these tour companies are listed in the Cuba Crib Sheet later in this book.

Given the difficulty of finding public transportation to some regions of Cuba, travelers who ordinarily would never consider a tour might change their mind in this case.

WORK

There are three ways in which a foreigner may work in Cuba. Idealists who are not worried about the next month's rent may volunteer with any of several "brigades" (see the Crib Sheet for contact numbers). This is not a bad idea for those who would like to work alongside Cubans in housing construction or agriculture.

Most people who are considering lengthy stays in Cuba would prefer to support themselves. A second alternative is to establish a business, a subject that has already been discussed in Chapter 5.

The third alternative is to find a source of dollars from your home country. Since the cost of living in Cuba is relatively cheap and dollars go a long way, even a minimal salary from your native country will suffice, at least to survive. Your own creativity is required here. Virtually every profession may have something to learn from Cuba. For example, a music school in your country of origin could pay you to make recordings of Cuban music groups. Your community newspaper might offer you a modest stipend for articles on your impressions of Cuba. Your teachers' union might have funds available for you to study Cuba's education system. The possibilities are endless.

PERSONAL SAFETY

What will happen if the Cuban government does not find successful measures to bridge the gap between those who have access to dollars and those who don't? Cuba is a relatively safe country, primarily because most people have a role in the society, and hardships are endured collectively. It is much safer to be out on the streets at night in Havana than in Caracas, Venezuela, Lima, Perú, or Mexico City.

Havana streets are dimly lit, and yet the one foreigner I know who was robbed in Cuba was pickpocketed at a brightly-lit dance in a glitzy hotel. Luckily, my friend from Holland had travel insurance that covered his loss.

According to an unclassified document from the U.S. State Department, "foreigners are prime targets for purse snatching, pickpocketing and thefts from hotel rooms, beaches, historic sites and other attractions." What the document does not say is more illuminating. Violent attacks and use of firearms in robberies are virtually non-existent; the streets of Havana are considerably safer than those of Washington, D.C.

If Cuba were suddenly to open its doors to an unbridled free market, class divisions would materialize quickly, and the personal safety situation would be likely to decay.

In the meantime, exercise the normal measures of caution. Don't flash expensive belongings. Don't put all your money in the same pocket or wallet. Walk on streets where there are many people (not hard to find in Cuba's cities at any hour of the day or night).

MEDICAL CARE

Emergency medical care in Cuba is free, and foreigners who must avail themselves of clinics and hospitals are charged quite reasonably. Travel insurance will only help in the case of a serious hospitalization.

Many people travel to Cuba for medical treatment. The Cubans call this "medical tourism." A list of Cuba's specialty clinics is found in the Crib Sheet.

Asistur is a government agency that gives assistance to tourists, including emergency medical care. Asistur's Havana office is open 24 hours a day, at Prado 254. Phones: 62-5519 and 63-8284.

If you have a health problem, ask for the nearest SERVIMED clinic (see the Cuba Crib Sheet). The U.S. embargo has caused a shortage of certain pharmaceutical products, so if you have a pre-existing condition, bring your medicine with you, including copies of prescriptions, in case customs authorities inquire about your medicines. Cuba has been able to produce some of its own medicines and medical equipment, and in some specialty areas, maintains state-of-the-art treatment that attracts "medical tourism." Cuban doctors may lack certain equipment or medicines, but they are as skilled and caring as the best doctors in the world. (See the Cuba Crib Sheet for specialties and locations of medical tourism.)

CLOTHING

The north coast of Cuba, including Havana, is not as oppressively hot as other tropical areas of Latin America, but it can be stifling during the summer. Winters are mild but a sweater and windbreaker are advisable. Informal dress is the custom, but remember that in spite of their informality Cubans are extremely neat and well-groomed.

IMPORTANT DOCUMENTS

Very few photocopy establishments are available to the public, and it would be wise to carry a photocopy of all important documents, such as your passport, visa, and airline tickets. In most countries, we are accustomed to finding photocopy stores all around town. Anticipate your photocopying needs in advance, and get the job done before you arrive in Cuba.

PHOTOGRAPHY

I have had no problem taking photographs wherever I please, and my daughter Siomara reports no restrictions either. Only military installations are off limits to photographers. Museums may have special regulations, so the visitor should inquire at the front desk. I've seen people taking photos at airports and train stations, but legally, rail and airport facilities are off limits to photographers.

Between noon and 4:00 p.m., light may be so strong as to alter the quality of color photographs for those who do not have the right filters.

TIPPING

Tips are not included in the bill. The tip is 10 percent. Most Cubans will offer help to visitors in need without expecting remuneration, but within the informal economy, hustlers expect a finders' fee.

THE INFORMAL ECONOMY

The Special Period has nurtured an informal economy, both legal and illegal. With laws in constant flux, it is virtually impossible to tell you in advance what is legal and what is not.

189

If you choose to do business with these "independent entrepreneurs," know in advance how to judge the quality of a product. If you don't like the hard sell you're getting, let the salesperson know that you are not accustomed to making a decision on a purchase under pressure.

Should you be considering the purchase of cigars, for example, read up in any one of the quality cigar magazines or books, so that you will know the difference between the counterfeit and the real product. Don't purchase a box of cigars without having it first opened. The box should have any number of labels, such as *Hecho en Cuba, Totalmente a mano*, and a Cuban government seal. The cigars should be uniform, firm, and the ringed label should be tight around the cigar.

None of these traits assure that the cigars are legitimate.

Before any purchase, visit the Palacio del Tabaco, Zulueta 106, between Refugio and Colón in Old Havana, where you can watch a cigar maker in action and inspect the particular cigar you have in mind. Black marketeers won't be carrying their product with them and will ask you to accompany them to their apartment. Typically, a box of 25 Cohibas that might sell between US $180 and $230 in a store may be obtained for as little as US $30 to $50 in the black market.

The ethical considerations of purchasing in the black market are perplexing. In some Latin American countries, the government purposely looks the other way and allows a thriving black market to exist, as a safety valve to prevent social upheaval. If government-run cigar factories are actually allowing employees to take a box or two of cigars occasionally as a fringe benefit, then there is indirect sanctioning of the black market. On the other hand, if these street cigars were stolen outright, there is no moral justification for purchasing them. Yet a third possibility exists. Black market cigars may be "seconds" or rejects. Who knows? A Cohiba or Montecristo reject may be a much better smoke than the cigars at the corner emporium in our country of origin.

EMOTIONAL CONTRADICTIONS

For some visitors, the most difficult aspect of adjusting to their stay in Cuba is the emotional bewilderment caused by constantly contradictory images and opinions, ranging from unfettered optimism to bitter cynicism.

The visitor to Cuba may be only minutes or seconds between sublime joy and heart-rending sadness. The best defense against the emotional roller coaster is to arrive without preconceived notions and then to accept the fact that life in Cuba unfolds with no simplistic answers.

CUBA CRIB SHEET

The Cuba Crib Sheet summarizes the most pertinent strategic visitors' information in a handy alphabetical format.

ADDRESSES AND PHONE NUMBERS

If you intend to phone or fax any of the numbers in this directory, Cuba's country code is 53 and Havana's city code is 7. A call or fax from abroad to Havana begins with the international operator code, followed by 53-7, and then the local phone number. If you are not residing in a hotel, international calls may be placed from major hotels such as Hotel Havana Libre, Hotel Inglaterra (near Parque Central), or Hotel Neptuno (Miramar).

Country code: 53

City codes:

Havana 7
Varadero 5
Viñales 8
Guantánamo 21
Bayamo 23
Holguín 24
Camagüey 32
Matanzas 52
Santiago de Cuba 226
Trinidad 419
Santa Clara 422

If writing to Cuba, especially Havana, after most addresses there is a line that names the nearest corner (*esquina*) or the two perpendicular cross streets, with the word for "between" (*entre*). Correspondence to most countries is efficient, but letter writing between Cuba and the United States is s-l-o-w and often a hit-and-miss proposition.

Cuba is a country in transformation. Even in countries where change is not the norm, addresses and phone numbers may change. There are no certainties, and we can only provide the most up-to-date information from the most reliable sources and hope for the best.

ASISTUR (FOR TOURIST ASSISTANCE)

Asistur is a government agency providing visitor assistance. This may include emergency medical care, repatriation, legal assistance, cash advances, finding lost luggage, new travel documents, reservations (cabarets, hotels, excursions, transportation, and cultural events), and insurance policies. This agency also works in conjunction with international travelers' assistance companies. Asistur's Havana address is Prado 254, Habana Vieja, on the corner of Animas and Trocadero. Phones: 62-5519, 63-8284, 33-8527; fax: 33-8087.

If you're outside of Havana and need assistance, Asistur will accept a collect call (*cobro revertido*).

BUSINESS DIRECTORY

U.S.–Cuba Trade and Economic Council: Yearly, weekly, and sometimes daily mutations in Cuba's business scene require potential investors to seek regular updates. The best source for business updates is the U.S.–Cuba Trade and Economic Council, and its president, John Kavulich. The New York phone number is (212) 246-1444, but callers will be encouraged to gather and update information on regulations and trends at the Council's web site: www.cubatrade.org.

Negocios en Cuba: This is the name of a high-quality business weekly published in Spanish, with critical articles, information on new business opportunities in Cuba, and a column called *Hecho en Cuba–Made in Cuba* with descriptions of export products. A yearly subscription costs US $40. Address: Prensa Latina: Negocios en Cuba, Calle E, no. 158, 4A, entre 9 y Calzada, Vedado, La Habana, Cuba. Phone: 33-8494; fax: 33-8495

Opciones, another weekly may become Cuba's version of the *Wall Street Journal*. Just how far have women progressed in Cuba? Four of the seven members of the editorial staff, including the director, are women, and seven of the eleven regional representatives are women as well. *Opciones* includes timely news, probing articles, business statistics, and a section of ads called *Propuestas de Negocios* (Business Propositions) with (1) export products; (2) business people in search of foreign partners; (3) industrial opportunities; (4) a weekly cultural calendar; and, surprise! ... (5) advertising, a novelty in Cuba. US $1 per issue and $60 for a year's foreign subscription (52 issues). Address: Semanario Opciones, Territorial y General Suárez, Plaza de la Revolución, Ciudad de La Habana, C.P. 10628, Cuba, Apartado postal 6344. Phone: 81-8934 and 82-0346; fax: 81-8621.

Note: when considering a subscription from abroad to either of these two publications, pick up a sample copy for evaluation from your nearest Cuban consulate.

Bolsa de Subcontratación (Subcontracting Exchange), a resource center for the latest industrial opportunities. Address: Edificio FOCSA, 1er piso, Apto. 1B, entre 17 and N Vedado, Ciudad de La Habana, Cuba. Phone: 30-9556; fax: 33-3303

Centro de Promoción de Inversiones MINVEC (a government intermediary arranging partnerships with foreign entrepreneurs). Avenida 1ra, no. 1404, entre 14 y 16 Miramar, Ciudad de La Habana, Cuba. Fax: 32-2105.

CEPEC, the Cuban government export department. Infanta no. 16, Vedado, Ciudad de La Habana, Cuba. Phone: 74-2185 and 74-2194; fax: 78-6234.

Consultoria Jurídica Internacional (International Legal Office) is an agency that guides foreign clients through bureaucratic procedures relating to business and personal needs, including contracts, documents on joint enterprises, registering brand names and patents, notary services, immigration papers, powers of attorney, and many other legal documents. It is staffed by attorneys, economists, and insurance specialists. Address: Calle 18 no. 120, esq 3ra Avenida, Miramar, Playa, Ciudad de La Habana, Cuba. Phone: 33-2490, 33-2697, 33-2861, 33-1368; fax: 33-2303.

CUSTOMS (WHAT CAN I BRING?)

Visitors are permitted to bring to Cuba, duty-free, for personal and not commercial use: personal jewelry, a camera, a movie or video camera, a portable CD or tape player with ten recordings, a portable tape recorder, a portable TV, a portable typewriter or word processor, a children's stroller, a tent and hiking equipment, medicines intended to last for the period of stay, two bottles of an alcoholic beverage, a reasonable amount of personal hygiene products, athletic equipment such as a bicycle, fishing gear, canoes or kayaks less than five meters long, two tennis racquets, and other sports equipment, and any other articles that do not exceed a value of 100 Cuban pesos. No food items allowed.

You're even allowed to bring in cigars for personal use, but who'd need that in Cuba?

But What Should I Bring?

If you plan on traveling to the back country, you might need mosquito repellent and anti-itch medication. Beach combers should bring sun screen. There's no law that says you have to bring a camera, and many seasoned travelers feel distracted by having to take pictures. But you will inevitably find good friends in Cuba; photographs will thus acquire a personal value transcending the scenery. With your camera, you're allowed to bring five rolls of film. Film is available in Cuba, and camera shops are found in most urban neighborhoods.

Other items you may need: an extra pair of glasses, an alarm clock, soap and detergent to save a trip to the store, tampons, standard medical needs, a plastic bag for soiled clothing, a Spanish-English dictionary, and a sweater or light jacket for the winter or even for the summer if you intend to sit in air-conditioned restaurants, where one can suddenly feel quite cold.

DISTANCES

If you are considering renting a car, cycling, or hiking, here are distances from Havana to many places of attraction in Cuba.

Baracoa .... 1069 km (663 mi.)
Bayamo .... 842 km (522 mi.)
Camagüey .... 570 km (354 mi.)

Cienfuegos .... 336 km (209 mi.)
Guantánamo .... 971 km (603 mi.)
Holguín .... 771 km (479 mi.)
Las Tunas .... 694 km (431 mi.)
Matanzas .... 101 km (63 mi.)
Pinar del Río .... 176 km (109 mi.)
Rancho Boyeros ...... 17 km (11 mi.)
Sancti Spíritus .... 386 km (240 mi.)
Santa Clara .... 300 km (186 mi.)
Santiago .... 876 km (544 mi.)
Soroa .... 95 km (59 mi.)
Trinidad .... 454 km (282 mi.)
Varadero .... 140 km (87 mi.)
Viñales .... 188 km (117 mi.)

DOCUMENTS

Tourists will be issued a tourist card/visa (US $25) by a travel agent specializing in Cuba or by the nearest Cuban consulate, upon presentation of a valid passport. Your passport is also a necessary document, and it is highly recommendable to carry a photocopy of the key pages of your passport in case it gets lost.

For long-term stays or more specific types of travel related to business or humanitarian organizations, consult your Cuban consulate. Travelers coming from the United States will need permission from the U.S. government if travel restrictions have not been lifted by the time you read this book. (See also **U.S. Travel Restrictions** in this chapter.)

GIFTS

If the U.S. trade embargo has not yet been lifted and you wish to bring gifts or medical supplies to Cuba, the proper and most efficient channel is through an authorized religious or humanitarian organization. Your travel agent will recommend the ones that are nearest your point of departure.

HOTELS

A hotel room may be reserved through a travel agent. Hotel rates will vary from agent to agent, depending on the cost of communication between the country of departure and Cuba. Until travel restrictions from the U.S. are lifted, it will be easy to get a hotel room upon arrival. Hotel reservations are written up on a voucher. The visitor may choose to have some or all meals included. High and low season varies depending on the hotel, and some hotels have no seasonal difference in cost. Most hotels will issue a "Hotel Card" (tarjeta *de huésped*) that identifies you as a guest. If you choose a hotel package that includes one or more meals, your hotel card must be presented when ordering food. Customary checkout time is 14:00 (2:00 p.m.).

In general, the less expensive the hotel, the more likely that visitors will have the opportunity to mix with Cubans on the premises. Cubans are acutely aware of this "tourist apartheid," and some are resentful. Architect Miguel Coyula, from the Group for the Integral Development of Havana, states flatly that "a person who has come to the tourist resort of Varadero has not seen Cuba."

Coyula's group is attempting to prevent what he refers to as the "Cancunization" of Cuba, and lobbies to maintain the eclectic appearance of the Havana skyline, while preventing architectural "mistakes" like hotels with tinted glass whose windows cannot be opened to a sea breeze.

I have listed hotels by city, with the letters from (A) to (D) indicating most to least expensive. The per-person rate goes down somewhat with double occupancy. Prices may and will change, but the with-breakfast, per-night, single-occupancy prices are as follows: A: above US $100; B: between $60 and $99; C: between $35 and $59; D: between $20 and $34. Two letters indicate that the price will vary from one category to another depending on the season.

Phone numbers are not listed since reservations should be made through your travel agent or from the tourist desk at any Cuban airport, where the host or hostess will tell you how to get there.

Havana

Melia Cohiba (A): spanking new, every imaginable luxury, located in the Vedado district.

Nacional (A): opulent, famous guests, a Vedado landmark.

Santa Isabel (A): superb location, Habana Vieja.

Sevilla (A): colonial architecture, pool, edge of Habana Vieja.

Riviera (B): pool, Malecón, Vedado district.

Plaza (B/C): perfect location for Parque Central, Centro Habana, and Habana Vieja.

Ambos Mundos (B/C): ideal location in Habana Vieja.

Havana Libre (B/C): largest hotel, convenient facilities, Vedado district.

Victoria (B): small pool, Vedado district.

Inglaterra (B/C): superb Parque Central location, rococco funk, balconies, Centro Habana.

Capri (B/C): back to the 1950s, Vedado district.

Colina (C/D): basic, comfortable, Vedado district.

Vedado (C/D): pool, Vedado district.

St. Johns (C/D): pool, Vedado district.

Deauville (C): pool, balconies, Malecón, Centro Habana.

Lincoln (B/C): a good deal, Centro Habana.

Valencia (C/D): colonial, serves Spanish paella, Habana Vieja.

Caribbean (D): basic, best bargain, good *ambiente*, between Centro and Habana Vieja, close to Malecón.

Like the Caribbean, the **Nueva York**, **Isla de Cuba**, and **Lido** are budget hotels where you're more likely to meet Cubans, and are all located in Centro Habana.

Hotels in Miramar are in the newest and most elegant part of Havana, like the **Copacabana** (B), the **Chateau Miramar** (A), **El**

Comodoro, and the less expensive **Residencia Universitaria**, but they're far from the action and you'll need a car or bike to get around.

Santiago

Upscale Santiago hotels have greater seasonal variations in price, with the highest prices usually in mid-January. Ask around for smaller, less expensive hotels that charge in Cuban pesos; foreigners may be allowed.

Casagrande (B/C): downtown elegance.

Santiago de Cuba (B/C, sometimes A): pool and view, east of downtown.

Versalles (C): south of downtown, on the way to the airport; you will need a car.

Gaviota (C/D): residential area, pool, east of downtown.

Las Américas (D): pool, east of downtown, good bargain.

San Juan (C/D): pool, east of downtown.

Trinidad and Other Historical Places

Trinidad is a UNESCO World Heritage Site. **Motel de las Cuevas** (D) is only a kilometer (0.62 miles) from town, with panoramic hillside views of both Trinidad and the sea.

Just outside of colonial Baracoa are two (D) hotels, **Hotel El Castillo**, with views of both bay and mountain, and the friendly **Hotel Porto Santo**, a stairway from the beach.

In Camagüey, the **Gran Hotel** (D) is as pleasant as they get, with a view of the city from an attractive restaurant and a cabaret.

Most of small-town Cuba is off the tourist track and attractive for those who want to slow down the pace and find affordable lodging. Remedios, host to the Las Parrandas festival, December 24–26, in the Province of Villa Clara, is an ideal example of an attractively-preserved colonial small town. A room in the more-than-century-old **Hotel Mascotte** goes for less than US $15.

Cuban resort hotel in Soroa.

Varadero and Resorts

Melia Las Americas, **Melia Varadero**, **Sol Palmeras**, and **Sol Club Las Sirenas** are all upscale resorts (A), each with facilities that rival any international resort.

Villa Tortuga (C/D) is a bargain spot in the vicinity of nightlife. **Villas Sotavento** (D) has common living room and patio. **Villa del Mar** (D), **Hotel Acuazul** (C), and **Hotel Siboney** (C) are among other reasonably-priced basic hotels that are worth it if you intend to be out of your room and at the beach most of the time.

Varadero has so many hotels and rooms that it might be better, if you're not in the high season, to get there and scout them out. Varadero is a beautiful site, but it is also a symbol of the contradictory scenario of tourism apartheid. Cubans are not permitted into many Varadero hotels, and the saddest part of this is when doormen make exceptions for prostitutes.

In fairness, Varadero is similar to other world-class resorts. Just across the Gulf of Mexico is Cancún, in a region known for the Mayan culture. Yet de facto segregation keeps the Mayans from the resort peninsula. The difference I've noted is that Cubans are more likely to resent Varadero than Mexicans are to resent Cancún.

Resorts

If you like a good resort but don't feel comfortable with the Club-Med philosophy, Cuba has a number of less overwhelming but nonetheless superb getaways.

At **Viñales**, in the province of Pinar del Río, Los Jazmines (D) has a large pool and stunning view of the valley of *mogotes* and tobacco fields. At **Soroa**, halfway between Havana and Viñales, within walking distance of a magnificent waterfall/swimming hole beneath tall shade trees, is Villa Soroa (D), with its own swimming pool and garden of orchids that grow naturally in the region. In few places in the world can one find such an inexpensive room in the middle of paradise, and we've just begun.

Author's daughter, center, chooses public beach, Playas del Este, instead of tourist enclave, and is treated to Cuba's racial harmony.

On **Isla de la Juventud** is the congenial Villa Gaviota (D), with pool and a mountain backdrop. Enjoy the slow pace and nearby scuba diving. At **Cayo Largo**, an island west of Isla de Juventud and south of Matanzas, the Hotel Isla del Sur (B) has all sorts of sports activities, including swimming, tennis, horseback riding, scuba diving, and deep-sea fishing. Both of these islands are reached by economical round-trip air fare from Havana.

In the ecotourist region only 18 km (11 miles) north of Trinidad, **Topes de Collantes** is a mountain rain forest health resort town, an escape for both Cubans and foreigners alike. Los Helechos (C/D) is a health club/hotel with a thermal swimming pool, gym, and sauna, and beautiful hikes to waterfalls.

Guardalavaca is the other Varadero, with every imaginable sea sport on the northern, Atlantic Ocean side of the island. Delta Las Brisas (A) is the most complete resort hotel, right on the beach.

This has been a selected list of hotels, covering the two largest cities in Cuba, as well as the major historical and resort sites. Thus far, Cuba's hotel building is ahead of the tourist rush, so if you're looking for hotels in places not on this list, you should have no trouble finding a room.

MEDICAL CARE

Health clinics are conveniently located in all inhabited areas of Cuba. Cubans receive free health care even for the most complex and costly operations, although certain key medicines produced only by U.S. companies or their foreign subsidiaries are not available because of the trade embargo. Foreigners are attended for free in emergencies but are expected to pay for other medical care, with costs usually moderate. Tourist hotels have free first-aid stations. An initial visit to a Cuban polyclinic is free.

No inoculations are required for travel to Cuba. The most common affliction of visitors to Cuba or any other developing country is travelers' diarrhea. By drinking bottled water only, you greatly reduce the risk of getting diarrhea. Using sunscreen, getting enough rest, and drinking plenty of non-caffeinated and non-alcoholic beverages are other preventive measures.

This author finds Cuba to be less disruptive to his digestive system than other Latin American countries, but readers will not appreciate such anecdotal information should they get sick after not taking sensible precautions.

MEDICAL TOURISM

Among the many people I sought out who have gone to Cuba for medical treatment, only one complained in any way, and his complaint involved being overcharged. I have no direct experience in receiving medical treatment in Cuba, so I am not in a position to make any recommendations.

I do know that Dr. Jorge Crisosto, the Chilean doctor who has done volunteer work in Cuba, when faced with deciding between Chile, Cuba, and the United States for sending his mother for cancer treatment, chose Cuba.

In 1996, Cuba received 5,365 patients, mostly Latin Americans, but including 1,218 Europeans and 92 Americans.

SERVIMED is the organization that oversees Cuba's facilities for health and medical treatment of foreigners. SERVIMED's Dr. Raúl Pría mentions Cuba's innovative treatments for night blindness, vitiligo, and neurological disorders. Ciro de Quadros, a Brazilian physician who works for the Pan American Health Organization in Washington, D.C., says that Cuban medical care in some fields like orthopedics is better than the rest of Latin America.

The main clinic for foreign medical visitors is Clínica Central "Cira García" in west Havana. Call SERVIMED for information. Some specialty clinics are listed below. For information on these and other clinics and health retreats, contact SERVIMED through your nearest Cuban consulate. The best strategy before considering serious treatment is to speak with people who have gone before you. Travel agencies specializing in Cuba are a good source for finding previous patients who have received treatment in Cuba.

For specific information, write to: SERVIMED, Calle 18, No. 4304 e/43 y 47, Playa, Apartado 16036, La Habana, Cuba. Fax: 33-2948; phone: 33-2658 or 33-2023.

Centro de Histoterapia Placentaria treats complicated skin disorders with a product derived from the human placenta. Dr. Carlos Miyares Cao is famous for his cures of skin disorders. Address: Apartado 16046, La Habana, Cuba. Fax: 22-4524.

Centro Internacional de Retinosis Pigmentaria "Camilo Cienfuegos" has personalized treatment for each patient to detain or reverse the process of the hereditary disease Pigmentary Retinosis. Address: Calle L entre Línea y 13, Vedado, Ciudad de la Habana, Cuba. Phone: 32-5554, 32-5555, 32-5597.

Hospital Clínico Quirúrgico "Hermanos Ameijeiras" has advanced techniques and a successful tradition of heart, lung, pancreas, and other transplants.

Centro de Microcirugía Oftálmica treats myopia, astigmatism, glaucoma, and cataracts.

Centro Iberoamericano de Trasplante y Regeneración del Sistema Nervioso does promising research in the treatment of Parkinson's disease and other nervous system disorders.

Centro Internacional de Restauración Neurológica (CIREN) has had promising results in treating Parkinson's and other nervous system maladies. Ave. 24 #15805, Playa, Ciudad de La Habana, Cuba. Fax: 33-6339, 33-6028.

Hospital Ortopédico Nacional.

Villa "El Quinqué" specializes in the treatment of addictions.

STUDY OPPORTUNITIES

Mercadu, Cuba's largest association specializing in study sojourns for foreigners, offers courses in a wide variety of fields and in different parts of Cuba. Intensive Spanish classes are held at the University of Havana. Mercadu also organizes many of Cuba's international conferences and symposiums.

For information on tuition, room and board, dates and subjects, and annual seminars, write to: Mercadu S.A., Calle 13 No. 951, esq Avenida 8, Vedado, Havana 23, Código Postal 12300, Cuba. Fax: 33-3028; phone: 33-3893.

La Escuela Nacional de Cine, Televisión y Video offers superb study programs. This author has interviewed several students and former students, including one of Bolivia's foremost film makers, Marcos Loayza. Public transportation to the facilities near San Antonio de Los Baños outside of Havana is irregular, but students are given free bus service to and from Havana. Write to: Escuela Nacional de Cine, Televisión y Video, Apartado Aereo 4041, San Antonio de los Baños, Provincia de La Habana, Cuba. Fax: 33-5341; phone: 0650-3152.

Oficina de Relaciones Internacionales del Instituto Superior de Arte offers courses in rhythm instruments, dance, and other arts-related subjects. My friend Serge took courses here and speaks highly of his experience. Courses are participatory, and dialogue between students, teachers, and guest artists is the norm. Write to: Oficina de Relaciones Internacionales, Instituto Superior del Arte, Calle 120, No. 1110, Cubanacán, Playa, Havana 12100. Fax: 33-6633; phone: 21-6075.

Grupo de Turismo Científico Educacional is in the beautiful Miramar neighborhood, near many of the foreign embassies. A variety of courses include intensive Spanish classes at **Centro de Idiomas Extranjeras José Martí**. Address: Calle 16, no. 109, Miramar, La Habana, Cuba. Fax: 33-1697.

One of thousands of foreign professionals attending conferences in Cuba, Dr. Birenda Das, from India, presented a paper on nuclear medicine.

Promotor Cultural, Casa del Caribe offers a chance to study in El Oriente, in historic Santiago. A wide variety of courses include Afro-Cuban subjects. Address: Calle 13 no. 154, Vista Alegre, Santiago de Cuba. Phone: 4-2285; fax: 4-2387.

Universidad de la Habana. I have interviewed several people who were quite happy with their studies at Cuba's foremost university. For up-to-date information, ask for an appointment with the nearest Cuban consul, and in the case of U.S. citizens, with Cuba's Foreign Interests Section in the Adams-Morgan neighborhood of Washington, D.C. (Fax: 202/797-8521; phone: 202/797-8518.) Also contact: Global Exchange, 2017 Mission St. #303, San Francisco, CA 94110. Phone: 1-800/497-1994; fax: 415/255-7498.

TOURS FOR PEOPLE WHO DON'T LIKE TOURS

Some of the best tour companies have direct communication with the above and other Cuban educational institutions serving foreigners.

The following tour agencies are the antithesis of the typical post-card-picture-snapping tour industry, and are geared for the highly sophisticated culture enthusiast.

In particular, several tour agencies operating from the United States deserve special commendation for enduring harassment from pro-embargo militants. The operations of these educational tour companies are painstakingly legal. Although politically "progressive," these organizations operate within a critical perspective, and they are very much people-oriented, so should you decide to travel this way, expect to have challenging dialogue with Cubans in your field of choice.

Global Exchange. This company operates what are called "reality tours" and specializes in public health, the arts, volunteer work groups, Afro-Cuban culture, eco-tourism, film, and other themes. A typical tour lasts from 10 days to two weeks and costs about US $1,350 from Cancún, México. One professional who made a tour with Global Exchange called it "the experience of a lifetime." Global Exchange also sponsors bicycle trips and studies through the University of Havana. Call 800/497-1994. Fax: 415/255-7498. Address: 2017 Mission St. #303, San Francisco, CA 94110.
Internet: www.globalexchange.org.
E-mail: gx-realitytours@globalexchange.org.

Marazul Tours. Here is another pioneer in tours to Cuba. One of Marazul's many specialties is the Cuban convention circuit. If you have a profession, Marazul will probably find a symposium, seminar, or convention to fit your needs. Marazul also publishes up-to-date strategic travel information for its clients. Write to Marazul Tours, Inc., Tower Plaza, 4100 Park Avenue, Weehawken, NJ 07087. Phone: 800/223-5334; fax: 201/319-9009.

Center for Cuban Studies. Operated by a veteran of the Venceremos Brigade and author of a book on Cuba, Sandra Levinson, this organization also publishes a bimonthly newsletter on Cuba. Unlike

Global Exchange, which travels to many parts of the world, the Center for Cuban Studies specializes in Cuba only. Many distinguished public figures and intellectuals are sponsors of the Center, including Harry Belafonte, Noam Chomsky, Francis Coppola, Jules Feiffer, and John Womack, Jr. Tours are similar in price and substance to those of Global Exchange. Write: Center for Cuban Studies, 124 West 23rd Street, New York, NY 10011. Fax: 212/242-1937; phone: 212/242-0559.

From Canada
Canadians will find many Cuba tour specialists advertised in the *Toronto Star* travel section. Two such agencies with package tours are: **Bel Air Travel**, phones: 800/465-4631 or 416/699-8833 and **Sun Holidays**, phones: 800/387-0571 or 416/322-0333.

From the UK
UK residents have a number of choices. A few include: **Havanatur** from Cuba operating in Surrey, phone: 44-181-681-3613/fax: 44-181-760-0031; **Progressuve Tours**, in London, phone: 44-171-262-1676; and **South American Experience**, in London, phone: 44-171-976-5511/fax: 44-171-976-6908.

From Other Countries
Havanatur operates from many other countries where English is spoken, including Holland (Havanatur Benelux), England (Regent Holiday Ltd.), Ireland (Cubatravel), Israel (Natour), Jamaica (Caribic Vacations Ltd.), Japan (Kyoei Havanatour Ltd.), and Switzerland (Jelmoli and Imholz).

Australia's most comprehensive cultural tour agency specializing in Cuba is The Cuba Company in Melbourne, phone: 03-9867-1200.

If your country was not mentioned here, your local Cuban consulate will direct you to the best Cuba tour specialists.

U.S. TRAVEL RESTRICTIONS

In case travel restrictions for U.S. citizens have not yet been lifted as you read these lines, consider the following legal scenario: "Technically" it is not illegal for U.S. citizens to travel to Cuba but it is illegal to spend money there. Many U.S. citizens take a chance and travel to Cuba, since Cuban immigration authorities do not stamp U.S. passports. When I once traveled out of Cuba, the immigration authority smiled and said, "Don't worry, I won't stamp your passport." It didn't matter to me though, since I had a license.

According to representatives of Marazul Tours, U.S. authorities stationed to meet arriving flights from Havana to Caribbean airports have harassed and sometimes charged U.S. citizens with disobeying travel restrictions, which has led to a few stiff fines. (I saw no such authorities at Cancún, nor did friends who arrived from Cuba via that same Mexican airport.)

The Helms-Burton Act raises the potential penalty on Americans who go to Cuba to $250,000 in criminal fines and $55,000 in civil fines. Between 1982 and 1987, the Treasury Department brought only 10 criminal indictments for various violations related to unlicensed travel to Cuba, and between 1994 and 1997, penalties of $1,500 to $2,000 have been assessed in 44 civil cases. One American artist I met in Havana claimed that "we have the right to travel wherever we damned well please according to the United States constitution, and I've been to Cuba seven times now with no harassment as yet."

U.S. citizens may obtain a license to travel to Cuba from: Licensing Division, U.S. Office of Foreign Assets Control, Department of the Treasury, 1500 Pennsylvania Avenue NW, Treasury Annex, Washington, D.C. 20220. Phone: 202/622-2480; fax: 202/622-1657. Internet: http://www.treas.gov/treasury/services/fac/fac.html

A "general license" to travel to Cuba may be applied for by government officials on official business, representatives of international organizations of which the U.S. is a member, persons whose stay in Cuba is fully-hosted and is not paid for by a person subject to

U.S. jurisdiction, journalists regularly working for a news reporting organization, and family visitors traveling once a year due to extreme humanitarian needs.

A "specific license" may be obtained by persons engaged in non-commercial professional research, freelance journalists, persons with clearly-defined educational objectives, members of human rights organizations, persons traveling for the purpose of importation, exportation, or transmission of information.

Usually, the permission restricts spending by U.S. citizens to no more than US $100 per day, excluding air fare.

VOLUNTEER WORK

Canada: Cuba Youth Tour, phone: 416/536-8901.

UK: International Work Brigade, 129 Seven Sisters Rd., London N7 7QG. Fax: 0171-561-0191.

USA: Venceremos Brigade, PO Box 7071, Oakland, CA 94601. Phone: 510/267-0606.

WEATHER

Cuba is a tropical country with an average of 330 days of sun per year. If you wish to avoid tropical rains, your probability improves by going during the months of December or August. Cuba is quite comfortable from November through March. Average annual temperature is 26°C (79°F) with the lowest average temperatures in January (23°C/73°F). The average relative humidity is about 80 percent.

WORK HOURS

Public offices are open from Monday through Friday, from 8:30 to 12:30 and from 13:30 to 17:30. The post office is open throughout the day beginning at 8:00 and closing at 18:00. Pharmacies are also open on a continuous basis until 17:00, with chosen (*de turno*) pharmacies taking turns staying open 24 hours.

CULTURAL QUIZ

"Experience is the worst teacher," said former baseball pitcher Vernon Law, "because it gives the test before presenting the lesson."

The intention of this cultural quiz is to provide a rehearsal lesson for some typical Cuban experiences before the real test begins, so that the reader may avoid having to learn the hard way!

SITUATION ONE

You are sitting on the Malecón sea wall in Havana and admiring the view when a total stranger begins talking to you. Within a few minutes of conversation, the stranger is asking personal questions. How do you respond?

A Tell the person "that's none of your business."

B Give partial answers if you are not comfortable sharing private information, and ask the same questions of your new acquaintance to see just how forthright he or she will be.

C Tell the person that you've got to be leaving for an appointment and that you hope to see him/her again some time.

D Respond frankly but with a meaningful context.

Comments

To foreigners from more private cultures, many Cubans, especially youth, are remarkably frank, to the point of seeming blunt, tactless, and socially indiscreet. Most observers judge this to be harmless and naive. If you answer either A or C, you are not willing to meet the people at least half way. Answer B buys you some time to feel out the sincerity of the person you've just met. Answer D is also acceptable, unless the question concerns something you'd want to hide from friends and family. For example, Cubans might ask you how much you earn in your country. If you simply answer $4,000 a month (a hypothetical amount), given the low wages in Cuba, you'll leave an impression that you're a member of the House of Windsor. But if you explain that you pay $500 for health insurance (Cubans pay nothing), $1000 for rent (Cubans pay no more than 10 percent of their salary), a dollar for two oranges (you can get 46 oranges in a Cuban outdoor market for a dollar), and $25 for a seat at a basketball game (sports events cost Cubans one peso), the listener will grasp that your salary conforms to the cost of living in your country.

SITUATION TWO

You've just arrived in Cuba and you want to feel a part of the country as fast as possible. Which is the best strategy?

A Visit as many parts of the city, and as many different provinces in the shortest period of time.

B Don't worry about seeing everything there is to see, and establish yourself in the neighborhood of your choice by patronizing the same establishments and hanging out on the same streets.

C Register to take classes or join a volunteer organization.

D Carry with you at all times a letter of presentation from the professional organization of your native country.

Comments

By "doing" all of Cuba in seven days and six nights (A), you'll end up with no lasting friends, and will not have established a sense of place. Most Cubans have not visited each and every city and province of their country, nor every tourist site in their city. Even if you were on a short visit, why gloss over everything superficially instead of getting to know a few people or places in a profound way.

D is also of little value, since oral communication supersedes written documents as a way to interact socially. B is the best answer, since Cuba is a country in which most things happen at the neighborhood level. C also makes sense, although it is not as necessary to join clubs or register for classes as it would be in more private and less spontaneous countries.

SITUATION THREE

Keeping up-to-date with the latest changes in business law, you have initiated the process to begin a business in Cuba, but the bureaucrat who represents your Cuban partner in the joint enterprise seems to be dragging his feet.

A   Invite him to dinner for a brainstorming session.

B   Offer a bribe by insinuating that you'd be willing to pay an extra fee to get the operation rolling.

C   Find a higher official in the government with more vitality.

D   Elaborate with your "partner" on the social benefits of your business for the Cuban people.

Comments

Unless things change radically, a bribe (B) is out of the question. Going to a higher-up (C) will be a damaging insult to the person you have been assigned to work with. Most Cuban technocrats are monitored closely and will do anything to produce documented results in order to advance in their profession, so try to work with your partner and not around him. Inviting him to dinner (A) is a universal strategy that works particularly well in Cuba. If he is indeed dragging his feet, he may need more evidence that your project will have social benefits for the Cuban population (D). Cuban officials are groping for ways to use certain aspects of the market economy to protect and improve their social advances, so ideas on how your business can help their goals will be appreciated.

SITUATION FOUR

It is mid-July and you have been invited to accompany a group of friends to an opening of an art exhibit at a Havana museum. How should you dress?

A   Dress informally, but wear clean, neatly pressed clothes.

B   Wear a light sport jacket with a shirt and tie, or a semi-formal

215

dress, and hope that you can bear the summer heat and humidity.

C It's too hot to dress formally. Dress comfortably like a hippie. These are artists and they'll understand your non-conformism.

D Phone the museum in advance and ask about the dress code for such occasions.

Comments

You could try D, but why waste a phone call to an employee who probably has no idea about any dress code. These may be artists, but the type of anarchistic bohemianism reminiscent of Toulouse-Lautrec is not the custom in Cuba, and sloppy attire (C) is not a fair way to honor the exhibiting artist. Nevertheless, in the heat of summer, no one is expected to dress up formally (B), which would be a vestige of nineteenth century colonial customs. A is clearly the best answer. One's personal hygiene, including neatness, is important to Cubans. Even during hard times when clothing was expensive and toiletry items scarce, Cubans found the way to be neat, fresh, and clean, even with informal dress.

SITUATION FIVE

You've rented a car and are on your way to discovering the Cuban countryside. You see a group of hitchhikers under a bridge or at the exit of a town. Should you give them a ride?

A Pass them by. They could be armed and dangerous.

B Pass them by. They will doubtlessly need to be driven into a town along your way, and you will lose time.

C Look them over as you approach. If they seem like family people or workers coming from or going to work, give them a ride.

D Ask the government official (called an *amarillo* because of his yellow uniform) if it's okay to offer a ride.

Comments

In Cuba, especially with the gas shortage-provoked limitations on public bus service, hitchhikers are a regular sight on the road, usually under highway overpasses or at the exits of towns.

There is no constitutional right to bear arms, since this would infringe on the public good, which supersedes individual rights, so the chances that your potential riders will be armed and dangerous are slim (A). Furthermore, if you're visiting Cuba to enjoy the people, then B is not likely a good answer, for a later arrival to your destination in exchange for meeting new people seems like a fair trade-off. Remember that Cubans are used to a great degree of uncertainty relating to arrival times. You will eventually feel uncomfortable trying to superimpose a tight but unrealistic schedule on the Cuban reality. (Rent the film *Guantanamera* if you don't believe me.)

This leaves us with answers C and D. Both answers represent ways in which the driver can exercise caution and still give a ride to hitchhikers. Once you see groups of people waiting together for a ride in the usual place for hitching, you'll realize that it is customary for drivers to pick them up, in what is called *hacer botella* (to hitchhike).

But to exercise the maximum degree of caution, D is the best answer. At unmarked but designated hitchhiking spots, you'll find a Cuban official with a notepad organizing rides and making sure that government vehicles required to give rides do so. With the OK from this *amarillo*, who will decide whose turn it is for the next ride, your safety is backed up by official sanction.

SITUATION SIX

You have heard about complex variations in how one addresses people in traditional Latin American cultures, according to social class, age, racial background, and region, and you fear committing a social faux-pas by being either too formal or too informal. What is the best practice to follow?

A It is better to err by being too formal. Always address people by their titles, and if not, with *señor* for "sir," etc.

B Address everyone informally, using their first name as soon as you know it, regardless of age or perceived social class.

C Listen to how they address you, and address them in the same way, especially when deciding between the formal "you" (*usted*) and the familiar "you" (*tú*).

D Be appropriately reserved when speaking with elders or those who appear to be of a high social class.

Comments

Cuba has discarded most formalities and social distinctions based on class, race, age, and region. A is not necessary, but you won't sound offensive if you use people's titles. D is also not necessary. If a Cuban is reserved, it is because he or she is inherently bashful, and not because of age or class distinctions. Both B and C are correct. In the case of C, some people in Cuba choose to use the formal *usted* while others immediately address people with the familiar *tú*. This represents a personal style of addressing people and not a social custom. The only obvious faux-pas you could commit is by using the formal *usted* with a person who has felt confident enough to address you with *tú*.

FURTHER READING

A BIBLIOGRAPHICAL COLLAGE

A traditional annotated bibliography about Cuba would fail to high-light the unbelievable disparity of opinions from apparently reputable sources. This thematic bibliography is structured around the very Cuban contradictions that readers will inevitably confront. In each of these "bipolar" bibliographical entries, the discrepancy between observations by two rational human beings may be so extreme as to become comical.

Given the controversial nature of this country study, I went beyond my own impressionistic experiences and anecdotal evidence, reading 75 books and more than 250 articles on the subject. We'd need a whole pamphlet for the entire bibliography. Some of the most noteworthy books and articles are noted on the following pages, while others have been cited and highlighted within the rest of the text.

Bicyclist in Viñales. With the fuel shortage following the implosion of the Soviet Union, Fidel Castro proclaimed "the era of the bicycle."

Bicycles

Oppenheimer, Andrés. *Castro's Final Hour: The Secret Story Behind the Downfall of Communist Cuba.* New York: Simon & Schuster, 1992, 246–247. Oppenheimer writes that "Castro's arguments in support of the austerity program were often bizarre ... Bicycles became his obsession. After *Granma* announced the importation of two hundred thousand of them—the first leg of a wider program of purchase— ... the Cuban leader proclaimed 'the era of the bicycle' had begun. Bicycles would solve most of the country's energy, pollution and health problems, he insisted in every speech."

Oppenheimer ridicules a *Bohemia* editorial for affirming that: "to expand the use of bicycles among us is an indication of cultural progress, a gesture of respect toward nature ... With bicycles, we will improve the quality of life in our society."

Waitzkin, Howard. "Primary Care in Cuba: Low- and High-technology Developments Pertinent to Family Medicine." *Journal of Family*

Practice. Sept 1997, 250–59. "The embargo apparently may exert some ironic positive effects in Cuba. Difficulties in obtaining petroleum products have motivated the importation of more than a million bicycles, which have markedly reduced traffic congestion and pollution and is probably improving the overall physical conditioning of the Cuban people."

Corruption

Wattenberg, David. "Smoke But No Cigar: A Traveler's Bad Experience in Cuba." *Forbes*. May 5, 1997, s53. "I almost didn't get out [of Cuba]. The uniformed Interior Ministry agent at the exit control booth suggested that I make a quick visit to the duty-free shop and purchase him a bottle of rum. Then he would be ever so glad to stamp my passport. I insisted that I was out of dollars. Finally he shrugged—it's Cuba, who isn't?—and waved me on."

Stanley, David. *Cuba: A Lonely Planet Survival Kit*. Australia: Lonely Planet, 1997, 81. "Don't even consider offering money to persons in official positions as a way of obtaining preferential treatment because—unlike the rest of Latin America—governmental corruption is extremely rare in Cuba, and you'll only make matters worse. If the police are interested in you, it isn't because they want to be paid off."

Demeanor

Mendoza, Tony. "Cuba Today: Instant Antiquity." *Chronicle of Higher Education*. Oct 24, 1997, B8–B9. "I was appalled by what I saw in Cuba. When you walk the streets you see faces that are as devastated as the buildings. People look depressed, beaten down. They stare into the distance, as if in a trance, as they wait for buses or in endless food lines, or when they sit on the sea wall, staring intently toward the horizon, toward Miami."

"Paraíso Perdido?" *Newsweek en Español.* July 2, 1997, 16–21. "Even though Havana presents an image similar to cities affected by wars, her inhabitants do not seem to be suffering. And the most important, they aren't under any pressure, but rather, they seem unworried ... It would be very difficult to explain where this enviable good humor and optimism come from ..."

"The cafes and bars where one can drink a beer or a soda are full of people. Amidst the badly-lit ruins, this exuberance shines fantas-magorically."

Economy

Hegeman, Roxana. "Exiles Prop Up Cuba." *Associated Press* wire article. Nov 28, 1997. The author quotes Amaury Alaguer, a Cuban exile publisher based in New Orleans. "Each day it gets worse. If you don't have dollars, you don't eat. And Cuba doesn't pay its workers with dollars. If you have pesos, you can't buy anything."

Whitelaw, Kevin, "Factoring in Healthy and Wise," *U.S. News & World Report*, June 21, 1997, 36. "... a new report released last week by the United Nations ranks Cuba *second* best among 78 developing nations on a new Human Poverty Index, even edging out Singapore and regional economic success Chile. Instead of measuring poverty strictly by income, the new index blends five indicators: literacy, life expectancy, access to health care and safe water, and the percentage of malnourished children. On that basis, Cuba has managed to maintain basic services and improve living standards for the poor, even though its economy has shrunk by a third since losing Soviet financial support in 1989."

Food production

Rosset, Peter and Benjamin, Medea. *The Greening of the Cuban Revolution: Cuba's Experiment with Organic Agriculture.* Australia: Ocean Press, 1994, 82. "If the Cuban people have been shown to be anything during the past three decades it is audacious ... what they have already achieved under conditions of extreme adversity is impressive. We are left with images of daughters and sons of peasant farmers producing cutting edge biotechnology, literally on the farm, and supplying their parents and neighbors with organic substitutes for toxic pesticides and chemical fertilizers."

Health Care

Waitzkin, Howard. "Primary Care in Cuba: Low- and High-technology Developments Pertinent to Family Medicine." *Journal of Family Practice*. Sept 1997, 250–259. "Cuba's physician-per-population ratio is 1 to 255, as compared with 1 to 430 in the United States ... The incidence of infectious diseases preventable by vaccines is lower than in any other nation at Cuba's level of economic development ... The Cuban medical profession is fully integrated in proportion to the racial distribution of the population, as opposed to the situation before the revolution, when the great majority of Cuban physicians were white. In addition, there is no evidence of racial barriers that inhibit patients' access to diagnostic, curative, or preventive services ... Financial barriers to health care access have been eliminated ... Cuba's isolation from the US clinical and research communities has prevented interchanges that would improve primary care services in both countries."

A United States Government official unclassified consular document on Cuba, 1997 states, "Medical care [in Cuba] does not meet U.S. standards. Many U.S. medications are unavailable."

Human Rights

Brady, Chris. "Back from the Future: Cuba Under Castro." *Science and Society*. Fall, 1997, 426–429. "Lithuanian human rights crusader Valdes Anelauskas told me that he and his confederates, who included anti-Castro exile Armando Valladares, made up or exaggerated incidents to impugn and destroy communism. Cuba's real human rights record is significantly innocuous compared to the rest of the region, even by bourgeois definitions."

"See No Evil." *The Economist*. Aug 2, 1997, 25. The maximo leader's "courts had recently awarded 18 months' imprisonment to two young Cubans for speaking their minds ... The two men already sent to prison, in April and June, were [members of] a group calling itself Young People for Democracy. They had already been sentenced to internal exile in mid-1996. Officially, their crime is 'disrespect' (in one case 'to the commander in chief,' Mr. Castro). Their real offense is to have called for freedom in the universities."

Schroth, Raymond. "Cuba Sinks Under Weight of Fidel's Dated Phobias. *National Catholic Reporter*. Sep 5, 1997, 10–11. "The Revolution executed 500 of its opponents in its first months, and Che himself justified the killings with a cold 'us or them' morality."

Stanley, David. *Cuba: A Lonely Planet Travel Survival Kit*. Australia: Lonely Planet, 1997, 36. Condemning the existence of "prisoners of conscience" and "summary executions," Stanley explains: "it must also be viewed in the context of a small country perpetually threatened with destabilization by a powerful neighbor. Unlike many other Latin American countries, there are no 'death squads' in Cuba carrying out extrajudicial murder, and lethal 'disappearances' off the street are unknown. Cases of torture during detention or sexual abuse of women by security forces are also extremely rare. Compared to countries like Colombia, Perú, Brazil, Guatemala, and Venezuela, Cuba's human rights record is good."

Santería

Most writers who visit Cuba are fascinated with Santería, and make attempts to decipher this magical religion. If you read one account it all seems pretty clear, until you read the next one. I can understand the confusion. After having visited several homes with prominently displayed *orishas* in their living rooms, I got confused myself.

Williams, Stephen. *Cuba: The Land, the History, the People, the Culture.* Philadelphia, Pennsylvania: Running Press, 1994, 82. Many writers disagree as to which is the top god. Some say it's Obatalá, but Williams writes that it's Olofi, and that "Obatalá ... was the first Orisha created by Olofi." Both Williams and Stanley (*Lonely Planet*) recognize the importance of Yemanyá. Stanley has her as goddess of the ocean and mother of all orishas, but she gets demoted by Williams, becoming only the patron saint of the ports of Havana and Matanzas (with no control over Miami, for example), and mother of only "fourteen of the most powerful orishas."

Kurlansky, Mark. "Havana 1990s: The Babalawos and the Birds." *The Readers' Companion to Cuba.* New York: Harcourt Brace, 1997, 345–353. One of the most fascinating accounts of a foreign visitor interacting with Santería is found in Mark Kurlansky's essay. Kurlansky associates Yemanyá (spellings of the gods change from source to source) as a replacement for the Blessed Virgin Mary, while Williams has her as Our Lady of Regla.

Vitality

Michener, James A. and Kings, John. *Six Days in Havana.* Austin, Texas: University of Texas Press, 1989. Michener made a career of traveling to different places and writing about them. But for many years, only Cuba was off limits to him. He felt "blocked on both ends," by a U.S. State Department that looked on with suspicion and a Cuban government that would suspect that a writer would report unfavorably. Michener sought an underlying truth that no one's hidden political agenda could refute. But there are lines and paragraphs in his book when even Michener fails to dodge the charged polemics.

However, in this bibliography of contrary opinions, only Michener's observation has no refutation from any side.

" ... the Cuban is a being apart, colorful, enterprising, and chock-full of verve, that regimes may come and go in different guises, but the essential Cuban will remain the same."

THE AUTHOR

Mark Cramer and his wife Martha decided at one point in their high-pressured existence that their common joy involved living in different cultures. Before anyone coined the term "simplicity movement," they embarked on a path of radical downward mobility, discarding their consumer luxuries (and what some people would consider necessities) that had tied them down.

Rather than skip around the world for photographic glimpses of great places, to be left only with faint traces of nostalgia, they settle down in communities where they establish roots and make lasting friendships. Mark's two books about the United States, *FunkyTowns USA* (1995), used as a text in several universities, and *Culture Shock! California* (1997) have rare vision that could only come from one who sees his native country after having lived abroad.

Mark has written two other books on Latin America — *Culture Shock! Bolivia* (1996) and *Culture Shock! Mexico* (1998). His credentials come from intense years of living, studying and working in Latin American countries, and a Ph.D. in Latin American literature and history.

INDEX

DATE DUE

FEB 2 1 1999	JAN 0 9 2007
MAR 1 0 1999	
MAY 1 3 1999	OCT 0 4 2008
AUG 2 8 1999	NOV 0 7 2009
NOV 2 2 1999	NOV 2 8 2009
APR 0 1 2000	NOV 2 8 2009
JAN 2 6 2001	DEC 1 9 2009
APR 1 2 2002 JUL 0 2 2002	
OCT 0 2 2002	DEC 1 9 2009
FEB 0 6 2003	JUL 2 3 2010
SEP 2 0 2003	DEC 1 4 2010
MAR 2 0 2006	JUL 0 6 2011
DEC 1 0 2003	MAR 0 6 2012
JAN 3 0 2014	JAN 3 1 2013